# HEALTHY
## *Keto*
# Air Fryer
## COOKBOOK

# HEALTHY
## *Keto*
# Air Fryer
## COOKBOOK

**Aaron Day**

ALPHA

**Publisher** Mike Sanders
**Editor** Christopher Stolle
**Art Director** William Thomas
**Compositor** Ayanna Lacey
**Photographer** Aaron Day
**Recipe Testers** Irena Kutza & Lexi Winder
**Proofreaders** Amy J. Schneider & Polly Zetterberg
**Indexer** Jessica McCurdy Crooks

First American Edition, 2021
Published in the United States by DK Publishing
6081 E. 82nd Street, Indianapolis, Indiana 46250

ISBN: 978-1-6156-4979-2
Library of Congress Catalog Number: 2020941373

**Note:** This publication contains the opinions and ideas of its authors. It is
intended to provide helpful and informative material on the subject matter
covered. It is sold with the understanding that the author(s) and publisher
are not engaged in rendering professional services in the book. If the
reader requires personal assistance or advice, a competent professional
should be consulted. The authors and publisher specifically disclaim any
responsibility for any liability, loss, or risk, personal or otherwise, which is
incurred as a consequence, directly or indirectly, of the use and
application of any of the contents of this book.

**Trademarks:** All terms mentioned in this book that are known to be or are
suspected of being trademarks or service marks have been appropriately
capitalized. Alpha Books, DK, and Penguin Random House LLC cannot
attest to the accuracy of this information. Use of a term in this book should
not be regarded as affecting the validity of any trademark or service mark.
DK books are available at special discounts when purchased in bulk for
sales promotions, premiums, fund-raising, or educational use. For details,
contact SpecialSales@dk.com.

Printed and bound in China

Author photo by Laura Barr
All other images © Dorling Kindersley Limited
For further information see: www.dkimages.com

For the curious
**www.dk.com**

# Contents

# Introduction

Air fryers are typically known for their low-fat frying capabilities. So you might wonder how a high-fat diet and a cookbook all about air fryers could work together. Don't worry: I was also initially confused until I realized the one main benefit to an air fryer for a ketogenic diet.

The keto diet isn't just about eating fat—it's about getting the right kinds of fat. When you're prioritizing the right kinds of fat, those foods tend to be more expensive. If you look at the difference in cost between regular deep-frying oils and grass-fed butter, you'll notice that using good-quality fats more sparingly is the key to keeping your food budget down and your quality of health up. Quality over quantity at its finest.

Without a doubt, the main benefit of an air fryer is to cook using less fat, and when good-quality fat costs so much more, using less becomes one of the best reasons to use an air fryer rather than deep frying. Plus, you can still get that crunchy texture to your food you can miss when removing carbs from your diet.

But you don't need refined carbs to make food crunchy. You just need an air fryer and, well, this cookbook.

At first, I was skeptical of air fryers, but after experimenting, crafting, and optimizing recipes, I was convinced. Just like I did, you'll discover that air fryers cook certain foods better than ovens. They can bake, fry, and grill—all while also keeping precious moisture intact.

Because air fryers are much smaller than ovens, they're perfect for small kitchens. This means they also preheat much quicker. Gone are the days when you had to wait 15 minutes for the oven to preheat. Air fryers are often preheated in as little as a few minutes and thus save more electricity.

Whether you've recently bought an air fryer or you're a seasoned air fryer chef, this cookbook will offer many meal possibilities you might not have even thought about before. From bread to desserts to crispy fried snacks and muffins—they're all possible using quality ingredients and a little creativity. Flip to any section in this book and I'll show you just what an air fryer can do for you on the keto diet.

Aaron Day

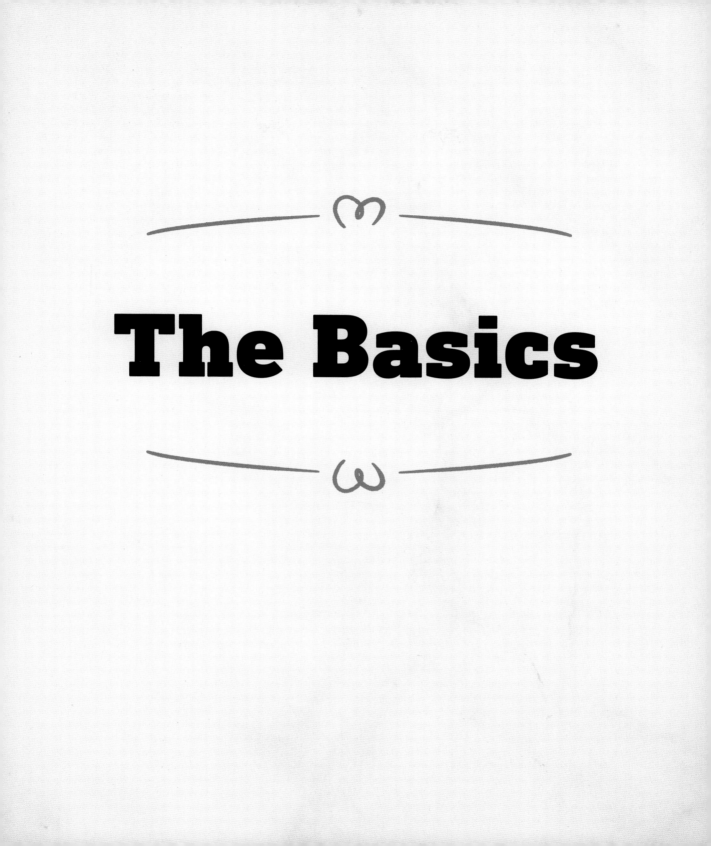

# The Basics

# What Is the Keto Diet?

Getting most of your energy from fat is the main principle of the ketogenic diet. For your body to use fat as energy, you need to reduce carbs from your diet because this is the first source your body will use for fuel. But this diet also has other health benefits.

## Keto basics

The keto diet has been around for decades, mostly as a treatment for epilepsy. It's now often used to improve body composition and possibly help reduce certain illnesses caused by excessive carb consumption. Most people get 50% or more of their daily calories from carbs, whereas a typical keto diet strives to use 5 to 10% of daily calories for energy. This reduction allows healthy fats to be burned for fuel in the body through the production of *ketones*—chemicals your liver makes, turning fat into energy—instead of being stored indefinitely.

## Macronutrient profile

On the keto diet, you typically get 75% of calories from fat, 20% from protein, and 5% from carbs. (The meals in this book denote how many net carbs and dietary fiber each recipe has. Add these two numbers together for the total carbs.) The carb restrictions required to induce *ketosis*—the metabolic state in which fat makes fuel—differs from person to person and often relies on such factors as insulin resistance, level of physical activity, and past dieting experiences. If you're unsure if the keto diet is right for you, consult your doctor, a nutritionist, or a dietitian for your specific nutrient requirements.

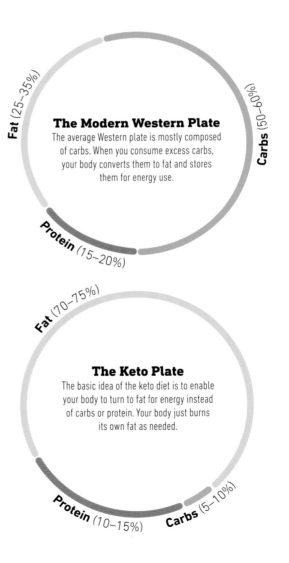

**Fat (25–35%)** **Carbs (50–60%)**

**The Modern Western Plate**
The average Western plate is mostly composed of carbs. When you consume excess carbs, your body converts them to fat and stores them for energy use.

**Protein (15–20%)**

**Fat (70–75%)**

**The Keto Plate**
The basic idea of the keto diet is to enable your body to turn to fat for energy instead of carbs or protein. Your body just burns its own fat as needed.

**Protein (10–15%)** **Carbs (5–10%)**

## Can the keto diet help with weight loss?

Being in a state of ketosis is often confused with being in a state of weight loss, which is often a by-product of eating a keto diet. Your metabolism will probably have turned to fat stores at the point of ketosis, but you don't have to be in ketosis or producing ketones for that to happen. However, following a keto diet can help facilitate a reduction in hunger and lower your need for a consistent source of food because of the metabolic adaptations made inside the body, which often lead to a reduction in body fat and improve insulin sensitivity.

Energy balance, macronutrient ratios, micronutrient balances, and metabolic health are all important factors in weight loss, so don't focus too much on being in a state of ketosis if weight loss is your primary goal. Speaking with a nutritionist who's experienced with low-carb diets is the best way to understand how to move effectively toward your goals.

## Is there such a thing as too much protein?

Protein is composed of many amino acids, which are used as building blocks in your body as well as sources of energy. Those building blocks are important for metabolic health, especially when physically active. A process called *gluconeogenesis*, in which excess amino acids are converted into glucose, can prevent you from reaching a deep level of ketosis.

If you're following a strict keto diet, working with your doctor or a nutrition specialist to find your protein threshold is important. If you're not following a strict keto diet, don't worry too much about protein affecting your level of ketosis because your body might meet its energy needs by burning protein instead of fat.

## Tips for keto success

Take these steps to ensure you stay on track, stay healthy, and reap the full benefits of following a keto diet.

**KEEP THINGS SIMPLE.** Start by replacing your regular breakfast with a keto-friendly one. Once you've done this for a week, then add a keto-friendly lunch and then progress to replacing all dinners and snacks with keto-friendly options. These gradual changes will ensure your body adjusts to the diet at a steady, sustainable pace.

**FIGHT THROUGH THE KETO FLU.** This isn't caused by a virus. The flu-like symptoms you might experience when you start a keto diet— lack of energy, intense cravings, thirst, fatigue, and irritability—are the side effects of your body adjusting and withdrawing from the glucose it depended on for years. Most people will experience these symptoms. But this isn't a serious medical condition and can usually be tolerated by staying hydrated, maintaining your electrolytes, and getting plenty of rest. Symptoms usually begin to disappear by the third or fourth day, so hang in there. You'll be amazed at how you feel afterward!

**RESIST CRAVINGS.** When your body is accustomed to consuming carbs for energy, it's used to a never-ending cycle of bursts of energy followed by crashes, but when your body is depleted of the carbs it craves, it can lead to some pretty significant cravings. Because cravings can be intense, consume a meal or snack that's high in fat or protein to help stave them. Other causes of cravings, like boredom, stress, and fatigue, can make us seek out a high-carb fix—even when we aren't hungry. Try to recognize these moments and look for another activity, like exercise, to divert your attention away from eating when you're not actually hungry.

**CREATE VARIETY IN YOUR MEALS.** Every chapter in this book has a great mix of recipes, so you won't feel like you're eating the same meal day after day. Eating a variety of snacks throughout a week can also keep you from getting bored with the same meals as well as staying satisfied between meals.

# Why Use an Air Fryer?

Air fryers use heat and circulating air to cook food. This means you can cook food with less fat than deep-frying in oil. That will allow you to still get a wonderful texture—even with the keto diet's restrictions on carbs. But cooking with an air fryer also has several other benefits.

## Healthier

When focusing on your health, you should avoid hydrogenated vegetable oils. If you're following a keto diet, using the right kind of fat—as opposed to less of it—is essential. Using a smaller amount of a healthy fat to get the same crispy exterior as you would when deep-frying makes air frying more convenient. You don't have to use an excessive amount of oil like you would for deep-frying. A small coating of healthy fat is all you need. Some healthy fats include olive oil, extra virgin olive oil, and coconut oil.

## More versatile

Just like an oven, you can bake, broil, and cook all types of foods with an air fryer. But unlike an oven, you'll always get a juicy piece of chicken or perfectly crispy bacon in less time because the cooking process allows the inside to stay juicy while the outside becomes crunchy. This means you can not only cook foods more quickly than in an oven, but you can also ensure even cooking.

## Easier cleanup

To clean your air fryer, simply remove the fryer basket and wipe with a damp cloth. For some foods, you might need a deeper clean by soaking or scrubbing the fryer basket. See the next page for some helpful hints for how to make cleanup even easier.

## Quicker and safer

You can often preheat the air fryer in a few minutes. Plus, food takes half the time to cook when compared with a conventional oven. Because the food is constantly surrounded by heated air, you can consistently cook food with a simple shake of the fryer basket or a quick flip of the food. Air fryers are also much safer than deep fryers because you're less likely to accidentally deep-fry your fingers in hot cooking oil.

# Tips and tricks

These suggestions will help you avoid many common mistakes made when cooking with your air fryer.

**USE A BAKING PAN.** A metal or silicone baking pan can help catch any dislodged items that might fall into the bottom of the air fryer, which requires cleaning. Baked foods like cakes or casseroles are especially best made in a baking pan—for easy removal and hassle-free cleaning.

**USE PARCHMENT PAPER.** If oils and juices accumulate in the bottom of the fryer basket, they can become hot and smoke or burn. To prevent this, place the food on a baking pan lined with parchment paper. This will also make for easier cleanup.

**SHAKE THE FRYER BASKET.** When air in the fryer doesn't have room to circulate completely, your food can often be cooked more on top than it is on the bottom. To avoid this problem, simply shake the fryer basket or flip the food halfway through the cooking time to ensure the food is cooked evenly and all the way through.

**PREHEAT THE AIR FRYER.** Preheating the air fryer and also coating the fryer basket with healthy cooking oil can help mitigate the risk of undercooked food or food sticking to the fryer basket. If your food does look a little undercooked even though the correct cooking time has been followed, just place the food back into the air fryer and cook for a few extra minutes at a time until your food is thoroughly cooked.

**USE NONSTICK COOKING SPRAY.** Some recipes include a nonstick cooking spray to prevent food from sticking to the fryer basket. You can use almost any cooking oil you prefer for the job, as long as it's not damaged at high heats (above 375°F (190°C). (Coconut oil is a great option.) The additional oil isn't included in the nutritional information because the nutritional differences are negligible to the final nutrition.

**CLEAN THE AIR FRYER.** Food and grease left at the bottom of the air fryer will often burn and smoke throughout the entire appliance if not removed with proper cleaning after each use. Use parchment paper or even a baking pan to help eliminate most of your cleaning troubles. Make sure to also check the fryer basket before preheating the air fryer to ensure the basket is clean.

**USE ALUMINUM FOIL SLINGS.** An aluminum foil sling can help you put a low-sided pan into the fryer basket as well as remove the pan once cooking is complete. To make a sling, fold a square piece of aluminum foil lengthwise a few times until you have a thin but strong piece of foil. Place the pan in the middle of that foil and lower the pan into the fryer basket using the ends of the foil as grips. Fold the foil back on itself once inside the air fryer so you can easily remove the pan without burning your hands or dropping the pan.

# Breakfasts

# Crustless Quiche Lorraine

Quiche Lorraine is a French savory custard-filled tart with bacon and cheese, but this version also uses ham for the crust instead of a wheat base.

**NUTRITION PER ½ QUICHE:**
**573** CALORIES
**48g** FAT
**5g** NET CARBS
**31g** PROTEIN
**1g** DIETARY FIBER

PREP TIME
**7 mins**

COOK TIME
**17 mins**

MAKES
**1 quiche**

SERVING SIZE
**½ quiche**

2 slices of bacon (3oz [90g])

6 slices of ham (3oz [90g])

2 large eggs

½ cup heavy whipping cream

¼ tsp paprika

¼ tsp ground nutmeg

½ tsp ground black pepper

½ cup plus ¼ cup grated Cheddar cheese

**1.** Set the air fryer temp to 350°F (175°C).

**2.** Place the bacon in the fryer basket and cook until crispy, about 5 minutes. Transfer the bacon to a plate to cool. Cut the bacon into small pieces. Set aside.

**3.** Cover the bottom of an 8-inch (20cm) baking dish with the ham by placing the slices in a circular motion. Set aside.

**4.** In a medium bowl, whisk together the eggs. Add the whipping cream, paprika, nutmeg, and pepper. Whisk until well combined.

**5.** Place a few pieces of bacon and the ½ cup of Cheddar cheese evenly on top of the ham. Pour the egg mixture over the top. Sprinkle the remaining ¼ cup of Cheddar cheese evenly over the egg mixture and top with the remaining bacon.

**6.** Place the dish in an aluminum foil sling (see page 13) and use the sling to place the dish in the fryer basket. Cook until the quiche is cooked all the way through, about 12 minutes. (Poke the middle and ensure the eggs feel cooked and not watery).

**7.** Remove the dish from the fryer basket and allow the quiche to cool for 5 minutes. Divide the quiche in half before serving.

 **Tips** Make sure the ham covers the entire baking dish so the quiche doesn't stick to the bottom of the pan. Add additional ham if you run out of coverage. Store the cooked quiche in an airtight container in the fridge for up to 4 days or in the freezer for up to 1 month.

# Avocado & Cheese Omelet

An omelet is a fantastic high-quality protein breakfast. This one is full of healthy fats, like oleic acid from avocado, and you'll love how creamy this meal tastes!

**NUTRITION PER ½ OMELET:**

**421** CALORIES
**35g** FAT
**3g** NET CARBS
**22g** PROTEIN
**3g** DIETARY FIBER

PREP TIME
**5 mins**

COOK TIME
**12 mins**

MAKES
**1 omelet**

SERVING SIZE
**½ omelet**

½ tsp olive oil

4 extra-large eggs

1 tbsp salted butter, melted

½ tsp sea salt

½ tsp ground black pepper

½ tsp dried basil

¼ cup spinach leaves

½ large avocado (3oz [90g]), sliced

½ cup grated Cheddar cheese

**1.** Set the air fryer temp to 350°F (175°C). Coat a medium-sized rimmed pizza pan with the olive oil.

**2.** In a medium bowl, whisk together the eggs and butter. Add the salt, pepper, and basil. Mix well.

**3.** Pour the mixture into the pan. Distribute the spinach and avocado evenly over the top of the omelet mixture. Sprinkle the cheese over the vegetables.

**4.** Use an aluminum foil sling (page 13) to place the pan in the fryer basket and cook until there's no movement in the center and no visible uncooked egg liquid, about 12 minutes. (Poke the middle and ensure the eggs feel cooked and not watery).

**5.** Remove the pan from the fryer basket and allow the omelet to cool for 5 minutes. Divide the omelet in half before serving.

**Tips** Store the cooked omelet in an airtight container in the fridge for up to 4 days or in the freezer for up to 1 month.

# Lemon & Blueberry Muffins

Lemon and blueberry combine in a sweet but healthy muffin for the perfect on-the-go breakfast. You'll love that these are portable and taste great warm or cold.

**NUTRITION PER 1 MUFFIN:**

**157** CALORIES
**14g** FAT
**5g** NET CARBS
**6g** PROTEIN
**3g** DIETARY FIBER

PREP TIME
**10 mins**

COOK TIME
**15 mins**

MAKES
**7 muffins**

SERVING SIZE
**1 muffin**

1 cup almond flour

1 tsp baking powder

2 large eggs

zest of 1 lemon

2 tbsp freshly squeezed lemon juice

¼ tsp liquid stevia

1 tsp pure vanilla extract

1 tsp olive oil

21 blueberries (about ⅓ cup)

**1.** Set the air fryer temp to 350°F (175°C).

**2.** In a medium bowl, combine the almond flour and baking powder. Mix well to ensure the baking powder is evenly distributed.

**3.** In a large bowl, whisk together the eggs, lemon zest and juice, stevia, and vanilla extract. Add the flour mixture and mix well.

**4.** Coat 7 silicone muffin liners with the olive oil. (Or use a large round silicone muffin tray. Using your index finger is the easiest way to spread the oil.) Fill each liner with 2 to 3 tablespoons of the muffin mixture and ensure the liners are evenly filled. Place 3 blueberries on top of each muffin mixture. Press the blueberries down until they're level with the mixture.

**5.** Place the muffin liners in the fryer basket. Ensure they're level and not squished from the sides. Bake until the tops have started to brown, about 17 minutes.

**6.** Remove the muffin liners from the fryer basket and allow the muffins to cool for 5 minutes before serving.

**Tips** Placing the muffin liners on a flat surface in the air fryer is important to getting nice-looking muffins. I placed the liners on a pizza pan and placed the pan in the fryer basket with an aluminum foil sling. (See page 13.) Store the cooled muffins in an airtight container in the fridge for up to 7 days and in the freezer for up to 1 month.

# Scotch Eggs

Scotch eggs are a perfect breakfast for a picnic, although they also work well as meal prep for the week. Hot air helps get the outside super crispy.

**NUTRITION PER 1 EGG:**

**373** CALORIES
**25g** TOTAL FAT
**6g** NET CARBS
**26g** PROTEIN
**1g** DIETARY FIBER

PREP TIME
**10 mins**

COOK TIME
**25 mins**

MAKES
**5 eggs**

SERVING SIZE
**1 egg**

5 large eggs

1lb (450g) ground sausage

1 tsp sea salt

1 tsp ground black pepper

1 tsp dried basil

¼ cup coconut flour

½ cup pork panko breadcrumbs (or ground pork rinds)

**1.** Set the air fryer temp to 260°F (130°C).

**2.** Place the whole eggs in the fryer basket and cook for 13 minutes. Transfer the eggs to a large bowl of cold water to cool. Remove the eggs from the water and discard the shells. Set the eggs aside.

**3.** Raise the air fryer temp to 350°F (175°C).

**4.** In a large bowl, combine the sausage, salt, pepper, and basil. Divide the mixture into 5 equally sized balls. Flatten each ball as much as possible with your hands. Place 1 hard-boiled egg on each sausage patty and wrap each egg completely with the sausage.

**5.** In a medium bowl, combine the coconut flour and pork panko breadcrumbs. Roll each covered egg in the mixture.

**6.** Place the eggs in the fryer basket and cook until the outsides are crispy and the meat has been cooked through, about 12 minutes, flipping the eggs halfway through the cooking.

**7.** Transfer the eggs to a platter and allow to cool for 5 minutes before slicing and serving.

 **Tips** If your local grocery store doesn't have pork panko breadcrumbs, place 1 cup of cooked pork crackling or pork rinds into a food processor and pulse 4 or 5 times. Store the cooked eggs in an airtight container in the fridge for up to 4 days or in the freezer for up to 1 month.

# Bacon & Egg Casserole

Bacon, red bell pepper, and onion enhance the flavor of this traditional casserole dish, replacing potatoes with cauliflower rice for a healthy, low-carb breakfast.

**NUTRITION PER ¼ CASSEROLE:**

**320** CALORIES
**23g** TOTAL FAT
**4g** NET CARBS
**22g** PROTEIN
**1g** DIETARY FIBER

PREP TIME
**10 mins**

COOK TIME
**30 mins**

MAKES
**1 casserole**

SERVING SIZE
**¼ casserole**

6 slices of bacon (3oz [90g]), diced

1 cup sliced mushrooms

¼ red onion, diced

½ red bell pepper, cubed

4 large eggs

1 cup frozen cauliflower rice

1 cup grated Cheddar cheese, divided

**1.** Set the air fryer temp to 400°F (200°C).

**2.** Place the bacon, mushrooms, onion, and bell pepper in a high-sided 8- to 9-inch (20 to 23cm) round baking dish.

**3.** Place the dish in the fryer basket and cook until the bacon becomes crispy and the mushrooms are wilted, about 5 minutes, stirring the mixture halfway through. Remove the dish from the fryer basket and set aside.

**4.** Lower the air fryer temp to 350°F (175°C).

**5.** In a medium bowl, whisk together the eggs until well combined. Add the cauliflower rice, ½ cup of Cheddar cheese, bacon, mushrooms, onion, and pepper. Mix well. Place the mixture in the same baking dish as before and cover with the remaining ½ cup of Cheddar cheese.

**6.** Place the dish in the fryer basket and cook for 25 to 30 minutes. Check for doneness by inserting a skewer into the middle. If the skewer comes out clean, the casserole is done.

**7.** Remove the dish from the fryer basket and allow the casserole to cool. Divide into 4 portions before serving.

 **Tips** Use an aluminum foil sling (see page 13) to place the dish in the fryer basket. Store the cooked casserole in an airtight container in the fridge for up to 4 days or in the freezer for up to 1 month.

# Chorizo Breakfast Hash

This delightful hash will give you a boost in thiamine, helping your cells convert food into energy, as well as selenium for healthy antioxidant function.

**NUTRITION PER 1 SERVING:**

**441** CALORIES
**34g** FAT
**3g** NET CARBS
**23g** PROTEIN
**3g** DIETARY FIBER

PREP TIME
**5 mins**

COOK TIME
**10 mins**

MAKES
**1 breakfast hash**

SERVING SIZE
**½ breakfast hash**

1 large red bell pepper, cubed

½ medium yellow or brown onion, diced

1 garlic clove, minced

1 tbsp olive oil

½ tsp sea salt

1 tsp ground black pepper

5oz (140g) chorizo sausage, sliced

4 large eggs

**1.** Set the air fryer temp to 400°F (200°C).

**2.** Place the bell pepper, onion, garlic, olive oil, salt, and pepper in a baking dish. Mix until the vegetables are well coated. Place the chorizo on top. Cover the dish with aluminum foil.

**3.** Place the dish in the fryer basket and cook for 4 minutes.

**4.** Remove the dish from the fryer basket and make 4 holes in the mixture. Crack an egg into each hole.

**5.** Return the dish to the fryer basket and cook for 5 minutes or until the eggs are done to your liking.

**6.** Remove the dish from the fryer basket and allow the hash to cool for 5 minutes. Divide the hash in half before serving.

**Tips** If the power of your air fryer is less than 1750W, you might need to cook the eggs for a little longer to ensure the egg whites are white and cooked through. Store the cooked hash in an airtight container in the fridge for up to 4 days or in the freezer for up to 1 month.

# Cinnamon & Egg Loaf

Egg loaf is a keto favorite. Eggs have a strong protein to healthy fat ratio and contain vitamin D, selenium, and B vitamins for energy and sustenance.

**NUTRITION PER 1 SLICE:**

**194** CALORIES
**17g** FAT
**2g** NET CARBS
**8g** PROTEIN
**1g** DIETARY FIBER

PREP TIME
**7 mins**

COOK TIME
**35 mins**

MAKES
**8 slices**

SERVING SIZE
**1 slice**

8oz (225g) cream cheese, room temperature

8 large eggs, room temperature

1 tbsp gelatin powder

2 tbsp cold water

2 tbsp hot water

1 tsp ground cinnamon

¼ tsp ground nutmeg

½ tsp liquid stevia

1 tbsp olive oil

**1.** Set the air fryer temp to 350°F (175°C).

**2.** In a large bowl, use a hand mixer to combine the cream cheese and eggs, adding 1 egg at a time until the mixture is smooth and without any lumps. Set aside.

**3.** In a small bowl, combine the gelatin powder and cold water. Allow the mixture to rest for 3 minutes. Add the hot water and mix until the liquid is clear and fluid. There should be no lumps left.

**4.** Add the gelatin mixture to the egg mixture. Add the cinnamon, nutmeg, and liquid stevia. Mix well.

**5.** Coat an 8-inch (20cm) square pan with the olive oil. Pour the mixture into the pan.

**6.** Place the pan in the fryer basket and cook until a skewer inserted in the middle comes out clean, about 35 minutes.

**7.** Remove the pan from the fryer basket and allow the loaf to cool for 10 minutes. Slice into 8 slices before serving.

 **Tips** If your eggs and cream cheese have just come out of the fridge, you can place them in warm water for 5 minutes to bring them up to room temperature quickly so you don't have to wait too long. Store the cooked loaf in an airtight container in the fridge for up to 4 days or in the freezer for up to 2 months.

# Cheese & Mushroom Egg Cups

Egg cups are a perfect portable breakfast option. Make a few batches for a nutritious breakfast you can reheat at work or eat as a super simple snack.

**NUTRITION PER 1 EGG CUP:**

**80** CALORIES
**6g** FAT
**1g** NET CARBS
**6g** PROTEIN
**1g** DIETARY FIBER

PREP TIME
**5 mins**

COOK TIME
**16 mins**

MAKES
**7 egg cups**

SERVING SIZE
**1 egg cup**

1 tsp olive oil

5 large eggs

½ tsp paprika

¼ tsp sea salt

½ tsp ground black pepper

3 medium white cap mushrooms (3oz [90g]), sliced

½ yellow bell pepper, cubed

½ cup grated Cheddar cheese

**1.** Set the air fryer temp to 350°F (175°C).

**2.** Coat 7 muffin liners with the olive oil. (Or use a large round silicone muffin tray. Using your index finger is the easiest way to spread the oil.)

**3.** In a medium bowl, whisk together the eggs, paprika, salt, and pepper. Place an equal amount of mushrooms, bell pepper, and Cheddar cheese in each liner. Fill each liner with the egg mixture.

**4.** Place the muffin liners in the fryer basket. Ensure they're level and not squished from the sides. Cook until the tops are darker in color and there's no movement or any uncooked egg mixture visible when lifted from the sides, about 16 minutes.

**5.** Remove the muffin liners from the fryer basket and allow the egg cups to cool for 5 minutes before serving.

 **Tips** Ensure the egg cups are cooked through before letting them cool. You can do this easily by pressing down on the edge of each egg cup to see if any liquid egg is below the surface. Place them back in the fryer basket for additional time if this is the case. Store the cooled egg cups in an airtight container in the fridge for up to 7 days or in the freezer for up to 1 month.

# Raspberry & Vanilla Pancakes

These are super easy to make but do take time. Have patience because these pancakes are delicious paired with fresh fruit and some sugar-free syrup and butter.

PREP TIME
**5 mins**

COOK TIME
**7 mins**

MAKES
**8 pancakes**

SERVING SIZE
**2 pancakes + 1oz (30g) raspberries + ½ tablespoon butter**

**NUTRITION PER 2 PANCAKES + 1oz (30g) RASPBERRIES + ½ TABLESPOON BUTTER:**

**400** CALORIES

**33g** TOTAL FAT

**9g** NET CARBS

**12g** PROTEIN

**6g** DIETARY FIBER

8oz (225g) cream cheese

½ cup coconut flour

¼ tsp liquid stevia

1 tbsp baking powder

1 tsp pure vanilla extract

4 large eggs

1 tsp olive oil

4oz (120g) fresh raspberries

2 tbsp salted butter

¼ cup sugar-free maple syrup (optional)

**1.** Set the air fryer temp to 350°F (175°C).

**2.** In a blender, combine the cream cheese, coconut flour, liquid stevia, baking powder, vanilla extract, and eggs. Blend until smooth. Set aside for 5 minutes to allow the flour to absorb the liquid.

**3.** Coat a sided 8.5-inch (22cm) round pan with the olive oil and place about ¼ cup of the batter in the pan to make 2 pancakes.

**4.** Place the pan in the fryer basket and cook until bubbles appear and the sides are easy to lift with a spatula, about 5 minutes. Flip, then cook until cooked all the way through, about 2 minutes more. Repeat this step for the remaining batter to make 8 total pancakes.

**5.** Transfer 2 pancakes to each of 4 plates. Serve each plate with 1 ounce (30g) of raspberries and ½ tablespoon of butter. Drizzle a little maple syrup over the top (if using).

**Tips** Don't worry if your pancake looks strange as you flip it because these pancakes will puff up more than a normal pan-fried pancake will. Store the cooked pancakes in an airtight container in the fridge for up to 7 days.

# Sweet "Bread" Pudding

My favorite dessert as a young kid, this tasty pudding will even put smiles on the faces of people who aren't following a ketogenic diet.

**NUTRITION PER 1 SLICE:**

**300** CALORIES
**22g** TOTAL FAT
**5g** NET CARBS
**22g** PROTEIN
**2g** DIETARY FIBER

PREP TIME
**10 mins**

COOK TIME
**22 mins**

MAKES
**10 slices**

SERVING SIZE
**1 slice**

2 tsp ground cinnamon

1 tsp ground ginger

½ cup erythritol (or ½ tsp liquid stevia)

1 loaf of Almond Flour Bread (page 96), cubed

1 cup heavy whipping cream

1 cup unsweetened almond milk

6 large eggs

1 tsp pure vanilla extract

2 tbsp cocoa nibs

**1.** Set the air fryer temp to 350°F (175°C).

**2.** In a small bowl, combine the cinnamon, ginger, and erythritol. Mix well.

**3.** Place 1 layer of Almond Flour Bread cubes in a high-sided 8.5-inch (22cm) round dish. Cover the bread with half the erythritol mixture. Place another layer of bread cubes on top and cover with the remaining erythritol mixture.

**4.** In a medium bowl, combine the whipping cream, almond milk, eggs, and vanilla extract. Pour this mixture over the bread and sprinkle the cocoa nibs over the top.

**5.** Place the dish in the fryer basket and cook for 22 minutes. Check for doneness by pressing into the sides and middle of the pudding to ensure it's cooked all the way through.

**6.** Remove the dish from the fryer basket and divide the pudding into 10 portions before serving.

**Tips** You can use any low-carb bread alternative for the Almond Flour Bread, as many grocery stores stock low-carb options that will work well in this recipe. Store the cooked pudding in an airtight container in the fridge for up to 7 days or in the freezer for up to 1 month.

# "Rice" Pudding

Instead of leftover rice, this recipe uses cauliflower and spices to bring you a healthy alternative that will keep you in ketosis throughout your morning.

**NUTRITION PER 1½ CUPS:**

**440** CALORIES
**41g** TOTAL FAT
**9g** NET CARBS
**6g** PROTEIN
**5g** DIETARY FIBER

PREP TIME
**5 mins**

COOK TIME
**10 mins**

MAKES
**3 cups**

SERVING SIZE
**1½ cups**

2 cups cauliflower rice

1 cup coconut cream

¼ tsp liquid stevia

1 tsp ground cinnamon

2 tsp pure vanilla extract

½ tsp sea salt

1 large egg yolk

**1.** Set the air fryer temp to 320°F (160°C).

**2.** In a large high-sided baking dish, combine the cauliflower rice, coconut cream, liquid stevia, cinnamon, and vanilla extract. Mix until uniform in color.

**3.** Place the dish in the fryer basket and cook until a slight brown color appears on top and the cream has thickened, about 10 minutes.

**4.** Remove the dish from the fryer basket and mix in the egg yolk until well combined. Place the pan back in the fryer basket and cook until thick, about 2 minutes more.

**5.** Remove the dish from the fryer basket and stir the pudding to ensure it's well mixed. Allow to cool slightly before serving.

 **Tips** Depending on the size of your cauliflower rice, you might need to increase the cooking time to allow the rice to become sufficiently cooked and tender to resemble rice. Before adding the egg yolk, cook the rice for 3 minutes at a time until the desired level of tenderness is reached. Store the cooked pudding in an airtight container in the fridge for up to 4 days or in the freezer for up to 2 weeks.

# Scrambled Eggs
## with Salmon & Avocado

Scrambling eggs in an air fryer is easy and delectable. Combined with healthy fats from avocado and smoked salmon, this dish is the perfect ketogenic breakfast.

**NUTRITION PER 2 EGGS:**

**480** CALORIES
**43g** TOTAL FAT
**3g** NET CARBS
**20g** PROTEIN
**2g** DIETARY FIBER

PREP TIME
**5 mins**

COOK TIME
**6 mins**

MAKES
**4 eggs**

SERVING SIZE
**2 eggs**

2oz (60g) salted butter
(½ stick), divided

4 large eggs

2 slices of cold-smoked
cooked salmon (2oz [60g])

1 whole avocado, sliced

5 chives, sliced

½ tsp sea salt

½ tsp ground black pepper

**1.** Set the air fryer temp to 350°F (175°C).

**2.** Place 1 ounce (30g) of butter in a sided baking dish. Place the dish in the fryer basket for 1 minute to brown the butter.

**3.** In a medium bowl, whisk together the eggs. Place the eggs in the dish in the air fryer and cook until soft and creamy, about 5 minutes, stirring every 1 minute.

**4.** Remove the dish from the fryer basket. Add the salmon, avocado, and remaining 1 ounce (30g) of butter to the dish. Stir to combine. Sprinkle the chives, salt, and pepper over the top before serving.

**Tips** Because the eggs will begin to cook after about 3 minutes in the air fryer, don't worry if you think they're not cooking immediately. Store the cooked eggs in an airtight container in the fridge for up to 5 days.

# French Toast

This sensationally warm, keto-friendly breakfast is made even more simple with the air fryer. This recipe is a comfort food just waiting for you to make it.

**NUTRITION PER 2 SLICES:**

**584** CALORIES
**41g** TOTAL FAT
**9g** NET CARBS
**46g** PROTEIN
**4g** DIETARY FIBER

PREP TIME
**5 mins**

COOK TIME
**20 mins**

MAKES
**4 slices**

SERVING SIZE
**2 slices**

2 large eggs

¼ tsp ground cinnamon

¼ cup unsweetened almond milk

10 drops of liquid stevia

1 tsp pure vanilla extract

4 slices of Cinnamon & Egg Loaf (page 24) or low-carb bread of your choice

1 tbsp powdered erythritol

**1.** Set the air fryer on the bake setting and at 400°F (200°C). Spray the fryer basket with avocado oil (or coconut oil).

**2.** In a large bowl, whisk together the eggs, cinnamon, almond milk, liquid stevia, and vanilla extract. Place each slice of Cinnamon & Egg Loaf in the egg mixture.

**3.** Working in batches, place 2 slices in the fryer basket and cook until browned, about 10 minutes, flipping halfway through.

**4.** Transfer the French toast to a platter and dust with the powdered erythritol before serving.

 **Tips** Because the nutritional information is based on the Cinnamon & Egg Loaf recipe in this book, you can adjust the numbers accordingly. Store the cooked French toast in an airtight container in the fridge for up to 7 days.

# Bacon & Egg Muffins

Why make regular bacon and eggs when you can turn them into ultra-portable muffins? This recipe is packed with protein, vitamins, and minerals.

**NUTRITION PER 1 MUFFIN:**

**95** CALORIES
**7g** FAT
**1g** NET CARBS
**7g** PROTEIN
**1g** DIETARY FIBER

PREP TIME
**5 mins**

COOK TIME
**15 mins**

MAKES
**6 muffins**

SERVING SIZE
**1 muffin**

6 slices of bacon (2oz [60g])

4 large eggs

1 tbsp heavy whipping cream

2 tbsp water

1 tsp ground black pepper

1 tsp onion flakes

½ tsp garlic powder (or 1 garlic clove, minced)

**1.** Set the air fryer temp to 400°F (200°C).

**2.** Place the bacon in the fryer basket and cook until browned but pliable, about 5 minutes. Remove the bacon from the fryer basket.

**3.** In a medium bowl, whisk together the eggs, whipping cream, water, pepper, onion flakes, and garlic powder. Line each muffin liner with a slice of bacon and then fill each liner with the egg mixture.

**4.** Place the muffin liners in the fryer basket. Ensure they're level and not squished from the sides. Cook until a fork poked into the side of an egg cup comes out clean, about 10 minutes. (Even though the top will look cooked, the underneath can sometimes take a little longer. If still uncooked, continue to cook in 1-minute intervals, checking for doneness each time.)

**5.** Transfer the muffin liners to a platter and allow the muffins to cool for 5 minutes before serving.

 **Tips** Don't worry if the bacon goes over the sides of the muffin liners a little. This will give the bacon a little extra time to become super crisp. Store the muffins in an airtight container in the fridge for up to 7 days or in the freezer for up to 1 month.

# Blueberry & Hazelnut Granola

This recipe creates a fantastic crunchy breakfast you can even make for the week ahead because it's easy to prepare, quick to cook, and portioned perfectly.

**NUTRITION PER 1oz (30g):**

**484** CALORIES
**46g** FAT
**7g** NET CARBS
**12g** PROTEIN
**6g** DIETARY FIBER

PREP TIME
**7 mins**

COOK TIME
**7 mins**

MAKES
**5oz (140oz)**

SERVING SIZE
**1oz (30g)**

½ cup almonds

¾ cup walnuts

¼ cup hazelnuts

⅓ cup almond flour

⅓ cup unsweetened desiccated coconut

1 tbsp unsweetened cocoa powder

1 large egg

⅓ cup salted butter, melted

¼ tsp liquid stevia

½ cup blueberries

5 cups unsweetened almond milk

**1.** Set the air fryer temp to 400°F (200°C).

**2.** Place all the ingredients except the blueberries and almond milk in a food processor. Pulse until roughly chopped and well combined. Pour the mixture into a high-sided baking dish.

**3.** Place the dish in the fryer basket and cook until golden brown and fragrant, about 7 minutes. Stir the granola every 2 minutes with a wooden spoon to ensure the top doesn't burn.

**4.** Remove the dish from the fryer basket and allow the granola to cool. Portion an equal amount of the granola into 5 bowls and top each with an equal amount of blueberries. Serve each bowl with 1 cup of almond milk.

**Tips** If you don't have a food processor, chop the almonds, walnuts, and hazelnuts into pieces, then mix the remaining ingredients in by hand in a large bowl. Store the cooked granola in an airtight container in a cool dark place for up to 5 days or in the fridge for up to 2 weeks.

# Hard-Boiled Eggs

Ever wondered if you could make hard-boiled eggs in an air fryer? This recipe gives you a way to effortlessly cook eggs without boiling a full pot of water.

**NUTRITION PER 1 EGG:**

**77** CALORIES
**5g** FAT
**1g** NET CARBS
**6g** PROTEIN
**0g** DIETARY FIBER

PREP TIME
**1 min**

COOK TIME
**16 mins**

MAKES
**5 eggs**

SERVING SIZE
**1 egg**

5 large eggs, cold

**1.** Set the air fryer temp to 260°F (130°C).

**2.** Place the whole eggs in the fryer basket and cook for 16 minutes. (Use a wire rack to elevate the eggs off the bottom of the basket.)

**3.** Transfer the eggs to a large bowl filled with ice-cold water. Allow the eggs to cool for 3 to 5 minutes before peeling. Serve immediately.

 **Tips** The air fryer used for this recipe is 1750W, so if your air fryer is less powerful, you'll likely need to increase the cook time by a few minutes. You can also set the air fryer to the bake setting. Try this recipe using 1 egg first, then increase when you're more confident with your own air fryer settings. Store the cooked eggs in an airtight container in the fridge for up to 5 days.

# Sausage Breakfast Sandwich

Why use regular bread when you can use sausage as the bread? This easy-to-make sandwich is perfect paired with a side of black coffee.

**NUTRITION PER 1 SANDWICH:**

**680** CALORIES
**55g** TOTAL FAT
**8g** NET CARBS
**30g** PROTEIN
**2g** DIETARY FIBER

PREP TIME
**5 mins**

COOK TIME
**15 mins**

MAKES
**2 sandwiches**

SERVING SIZE
**1 sandwich**

9oz (255g) ground sausage

2 large eggs

½ large avocado, sliced

2 slices of Cheddar cheese (1oz [30g])

2 tsp mustard

½ tsp sea salt

½ tsp ground black pepper

**1.** Set the air fryer temp to 350°F (175°C). Spray 2 egg rings with nonstick cooking spray.

**2.** Use clean hands to form the ground sausage into 4 large patties.

**3.** Place the patties in the fryer basket and cook until cooked through, about 10 minutes.

**4.** Transfer the patties to a platter and set aside.

**5.** Place the egg rings on a baking dish. Place 1 egg in each ring.

**6.** Place the dish in the fryer basket and cook until the eggs have hard whites and slightly runny yolks or they're cooked to your liking, about 5 minutes.

**7.** Transfer each egg to a sausage patty. Top each egg with half the avocado and 1 slice of cheese.

**8.** Cover one side of each remaining patty with 1 teaspoon of mustard. Season each patty with equal amounts of salt and pepper. Place each patty on top of each egg, avocado, and cheese stack. Serve immediately.

 **Tips** Making the sausage patties slightly larger than the egg rings is the key to a well-stacked breakfast sandwich. Store the cooked sandwiches in an airtight container in the fridge for up to 4 days.

# Mushroom & Spinach Frittata

This fantastic breakfast is made easy with an air fryer. Packed with fiber, vitamins, and minerals, this frittata will keep you satisfied throughout your day.

**NUTRITION PER ¼ FRITTATA:**
**290** CALORIES
**24g** TOTAL FAT
**4g** NET CARBS
**15g** PROTEIN
**1g** DIETARY FIBER

PREP TIME
**5 mins**

COOK TIME
**20 mins**

MAKES
**1 frittata**

SERVING SIZE
**¼ frittata**

¼ yellow onion, diced

4oz (120g) button mushrooms, sliced

2oz (60g) salted butter (about ½ stick)

2 cups baby spinach

4 large eggs

3 tbsp unsweetened almond milk

1 tsp garlic powder

1 tsp paprika

1 cup grated Cheddar cheese, divided

**1.** Set the air fryer temp to 350°F (175°C).

**2.** In a high-sided baking dish, combine the onion, mushrooms, butter, and spinach.

**3.** Place the dish in the fryer basket and cook until the mushrooms have slightly wilted and the onion is translucent, about 3 minutes, stirring halfway through.

**4.** In a medium bowl, whisk together the eggs, almond milk, garlic powder, paprika, and ½ cup of Cheddar cheese.

**5.** Remove the dish from the fryer basket and spread the vegetables evenly around the dish. Pour the egg and cheese mixture over the top. Cover with the remaining ½ cup of Cheddar cheese.

**6.** Return the dish to the fryer basket and cook until all the eggs are cooked through on the sides and in the middle, about 20 minutes.

**7.** Remove the dish from the fryer basket and divide the frittata into 4 portions before serving.

 **Tips** Use a knife or a skewer to check for doneness in the middle and on the edges of the frittata, as the top can cook faster than the bottom, especially if there's limited air circulation around the dish. Store the cooked frittata in an airtight container in the fridge for up to 7 days or in the freezer for up to 2 months.

# Cauliflower Bake

This bake combines the flavors of whipping cream, bacon, and eggs with the fiber of cauliflower to give this dish more volume to keep you feeling satisfied.

NUTRITION PER ½ CUP:

**120** CALORIES
**9g** TOTAL FAT
**2g** NET CARBS
**7g** PROTEIN
**1g** DIETARY FIBER

PREP TIME
**7 mins**

COOK TIME
**23 mins**

MAKES
**6 cups**

SERVING SIZE
**½ cup**

2 slices of bacon

4 large eggs

1 tsp paprika

1 tsp sea salt

1 tsp ground black pepper

1 chicken stock cube, crumbled

¼ cup heavy whipping cream

2 cups cauliflower rice (10oz [285g])

1 cup grated Cheddar cheese, divided

1 tsp salted butter

**1.** Set the air fryer temp to 350°F (175°C).

**2.** Place the bacon in the fryer basket and cook until crispy, about 5 minutes. Remove the bacon from the air fryer. Dice and set aside.

**3.** In a medium bowl, whisk together the eggs, paprika, salt, pepper, chicken stock cube, and whipping cream. Add the cauliflower rice and ½ cup of Cheddar cheese. Mix well.

**4.** Coat a high-sided 8.5-inch (22cm) baking pan with the butter. Place the cauliflower mixture in the pan and top with the remaining ½ cup of Cheddar cheese.

**5.** Place the pan in the fryer basket and cook for 17 minutes. Check for doneness by using a knife to poke the sides of the dish to ensure no uncooked egg mixture is underneath the top layer. Use a skewer to poke the middle to ensure there's no uncooked egg mixture.

**6.** Remove the pan from the fryer basket and divide the bake into 6 portions before serving.

 **Tips** If your baking pan doesn't have handles, you can use an aluminum foil sling (see page 13) to place the pan in the fryer basket. Store the cooked cauliflower bake in an airtight container in the fridge for up to 4 days or in the freezer for up to 1 month.

# Zucchini Fritters

Zucchini is high in antioxidants and vitamin A. This recipe will give your immune system a boost but also help avoid high-carb content that can halt fat burning.

**NUTRITION PER 2 FRITTERS:**

**108** CALORIES
**6g** FAT
**4g** NET CARBS
**7g** PROTEIN
**1g** DIETARY FIBER

PREP TIME
**35 mins**

COOK TIME
**24 mins**

MAKES
**14 fritters**

SERVING SIZE
**2 fritters**

6 large zucchini (21oz [600g]), grated

2 tsp sea salt

1½ cups grated Parmesan cheese

2 large eggs

1 tsp ground black pepper

1 tsp paprika

1 tsp dried basil

**1.** Trim and grate the zucchini. Place in a large colander. Sprinkle the salt evenly over the top. Set aside for 30 minutes to allow the zucchini to soften and the salt to help draw out water.

**2.** Set the air fryer temp to 350°F (175°C).

**3.** Attempt to remove as much water as possible from the zucchini by pressing the mixture into the colander over a large bowl or placing the zucchini into a clean cheesecloth and squeezing. Remove as much water as possible before continuing.

**4.** In a large bowl, combine the zucchini, Parmesan, eggs, pepper, paprika, and basil. Use your hands to mix the ingredients. Make 14 equally sized fritters.

**5.** Working in batches, place 7 or 8 fritters in the fryer basket and cook until cooked all the way through, about 12 minutes.

**6.** Transfer the fritters to a platter and allow to cool before serving.

 **Tips** Using cheesecloth to squeeze the water from the zucchini is ideal, but I've also used my hands with a relative amount of success. If there's still additional water when placing the fritters in the fryer basket, place them in a raised basket or on a wire rack to allow the water to drain. Store the cooked fritters in an airtight container in the fridge for up to 7 days or in the freezer for up to 2 months.

# Mains

# Shrimp & Chorizo Skewers

Shrimp and chorizo are an absolutely wonderful combo. Adding a side of green beans will turn this recipe into a staple Sunday afternoon main meal.

| PREP TIME | COOK TIME | MAKES | SERVING SIZE |
|---|---|---|---|
| **5 mins** | **10 mins** | **4 skewers** | **2 skewers + ½ the green beans** |

**NUTRITION PER 2 SKEWERS + ½ THE GREEN BEANS:**

**300** CALORIES
**22g** TOTAL FAT
**6g** NET CARBS
**20g** PROTEIN
**1g** DIETARY FIBER

5oz (140g) chorizo

3oz (90g) shrimp (about 10), peeled and deveined

2 tbsp olive oil, divided

1 tsp balsamic vinegar

½ tsp dried parsley

½ tsp dried basil

½ tsp sea salt

½ tsp ground black pepper

5oz (140g) green beans, washed and trimmed

**1.** Set the air fryer temp to 350°F (175°C).

**2.** Cut the chorizo into 10 pieces, each about 1 inch [2.5cm] thick. Alternate threading an equal amount of the chorizo and shrimp on 4 skewers.

**3.** In a small bowl, combine 1 tablespoon of olive oil, balsamic vinegar, parsley, basil, salt, and pepper. Mix well. Brush half the mixture on the skewers.

**4.** Place the green beans in the fryer basket and cover with the remaining 1 tablespoon of olive oil. Shake the basket to coat. Place a skewer stand on top of the beans and place the skewers on the stand. Cook until the chorizo is slightly browned, about 5 minutes.

**5.** Remove the basket from the air fryer. Turn the skewers over and brush with the remaining olive oil mixture. Place the basket back in the air fryer and cook until the shrimp and chorizo are browned on both sides, about 5 minutes more.

**6.** Transfer the skewers and green beans to separate platters. Serve immediately.

**Tips** Brushing the olive oil marinade works best with a pastry brush, but you can also use sprigs of fresh herbs for extra flavor. Skewer stands are usually metal squares with spaces on which to rest the skewers. Store the cooked skewers in an airtight container in the fridge for up to 4 days or in the freezer for up to 1 month.

# Lemon & Butter Salmon

Simple recipes like this are perfect midweek dinners you can pair with a fresh salad or various vegetables. Salmon is packed with omega 3, DHA, and EPA fats.

**NUTRITION PER 1 SLICE OF SALMON:**

**290** CALORIES
**20g** TOTAL FAT
**1g** NET CARBS
**26g** PROTEIN
**1g** DIETARY FIBER

PREP TIME
**5 mins**

COOK TIME
**8 mins**

MAKES
**2 slices of salmon**

SERVING SIZE
**1 slice of salmon**

2 skinless salmon fillets (4oz [120g])

1 tsp sea salt

1 tsp ground black pepper

2 tbsp salted butter

2 lemon wedges

**1.** Set the air fryer temp to 400°F (200°C).

**2.** Cut 2 sheets of 10-inch-square (25cm square) aluminum foil. Place each salmon fillet in the middle of the shiny side of a sheet.

**3.** Season each fillet with an equal amount of salt and pepper. Place 1 tablespoon of butter and 1 lemon wedge next to each fillet. Wrap the salmon in the foil and squeeze the top and bottom shut tightly.

**4.** Place the foil packets in the fryer basket and cook until the salmon skin is light pink all the way around and flakes easily, about 8 minutes.

**5.** Remove the packets from the fryer basket and allow the salmon to cool for 5 minutes sealed in the foil. Unwrap and serve with your favorite sides.

**Tips** A handy tip for easy meal prep is to freeze many of these portions of salmon wrapped in foil with the lemon and butter and then place them in the fryer basket straight from the freezer. Adjust the cooking time to 20 to 25 minutes for a fully frozen piece. Store the cooked salmon in an airtight container in the fridge for up to 4 days or in the freezer for up to 1 month.

# Salmon
## with Fennel Salad

Salmon and fennel are two flavors that complement each other well. This dish is a tasty and fresh main meal perfect for the warmer months of the year.

**NUTRITION PER
1 SALMON FILLET
+ ¾ CUP GREENS
+ 1¼ TABLESPOONS
DRESSING:**

**320** CALORIES
**22g** TOTAL FAT
**2g** NET CARBS
**26g** PROTEIN
**2g** DIETARY FIBER

PREP TIME
**5 mins**

COOK TIME
**10 mins**

MAKES
**4 salmon fillets**

SERVING SIZE
**1 salmon fillet
+ ¾ cup greens
+ 1¼ tablespoons
dressing**

4 skin-on salmon fillets
 (14oz [400g])

4oz (120g) fennel bulb, sliced

3 cups mixed lettuce greens

2 tsp balsamic vinegar

4 tbsp olive oil

1 tsp sea salt

1 tsp ground black pepper

**1.** Set the air fryer temp to 400°F (200°C). Spray the fryer basket with avocado oil.

**2.** Place the salmon skin side up in the fryer basket and cook until the skin is crispy, light pink all the way around, and flakes easily, about 10 minutes.

**3.** Use a mandoline or knife to cut the fennel bulb into thin slices. Place the slices and the mixed greens in a large bowl.

**4.** In a small container, combine the balsamic vinegar, olive oil, salt, and pepper. Cover and shake until the vinegar has emulsified with the oil. Drizzle over the mixed greens and fennel. Toss well to coat.

**5.** Transfer the salmon to a platter and serve with the mixed greens.

 **Tips** If you don't like the anise flavor of fennel, use small slices of celery instead to achieve a similar texture and crunch. Store the cooked salmon in an airtight container in the fridge for up to 4 days. Store the salad in an airtight container in the fridge for up to 24 hours.

# Whole Roasted Chicken

Yes, you can roast an entire chicken in your air fryer. This is a fantastic way to cook chicken because it prevents the meat from drying out.

**NUTRITION PER ¼ CHICKEN:**

**422** CALORIES
**27g** TOTAL FAT
**0g** NET CARBS
**41g** PROTEIN
**1g** DIETARY FIBER

PREP TIME
**10 mins**

COOK TIME
**50 mins**

MAKES
**1 chicken**

SERVING SIZE
**¼ chicken**

2 tsp ground paprika
½ tsp dried oregano
1 tsp dried basil
1 tsp dried parsley
1 tsp sea salt
1 tsp ground black pepper
2 tbsp olive oil
3lb (1½kg) whole chicken

**1.** Set the air fryer temp to 350°F (175°C).

**2.** In a small bowl, combine the paprika, oregano, basil, parsley, salt, pepper, and olive oil. Use a pastry brush to brush the chicken with the mixture until well coated.

**3.** Place the chicken breast side down in the fryer basket and cook for 40 minutes. Flip the chicken over and cook for 10 minutes more. Check for doneness by ensuring the chicken has reached an internal temperature of 165°F (75°C) and no pink sections are visible.

**4.** Transfer the chicken to a platter. Serve immediately with your favorite sides.

**Tips** For an extra juicy chicken, marinate the whole chicken in 2 cups of buttermilk overnight in the fridge. Separate and store the cooked chicken in an airtight container in the fridge for up to 4 days or in the freezer for up to 1 month.

# Chicken Nuggets

Crispy homemade chicken nuggets are easy to make with an air fryer. This recipe uses coconut flour—instead of typical breading—to create a crispy exterior.

**NUTRITION PER 8 NUGGETS:**

**295** CALORIES
**17g** TOTAL FAT
**2g** NET CARBS
**41g** PROTEIN
**2g** DIETARY FIBER

| PREP TIME | COOK TIME | MAKES | SERVING SIZE |
|---|---|---|---|
| **5 mins** | **20 mins** | **16 nuggets** | **8 nuggets** |

2 boneless, skinless chicken breasts (1lb [450g])

1 tsp sea salt

1 tsp olive oil

¼ cup coconut flour

1 tsp ground ginger

1 tbsp chopped fresh parsley

1 large egg

**1.** Set the air fryer temp to 400°F (200°C). Spray the fryer basket with olive oil.

**2.** Cut the chicken breasts into 16 nugget-sized chunks. Use paper towels to dry the chicken as much as possible.

**3.** In a large bowl, combine the chicken, salt, and olive oil. Mix well to coat. Set aside.

**4.** In a medium bowl, combine the coconut flour, ginger, and parsley. Mix until uniform in color.

**5.** In a small bowl, whisk the egg. Dip each nugget in the egg and then in the coconut flour. Ensure an even coating on each nugget.

**6.** Working in batches, place 8 nuggets in the fryer basket and cook until firm, about 10 minutes, flipping halfway through. (Ensure the nuggets don't touch so they get extra crispy.)

**7.** Transfer the nuggets to a platter and serve immediately.

 **Tip** Store the cooked nuggets in the fridge for up to 4 days or in the freezer for up to 1 month.

# Chicken Fillet Pizzas

This simple yet delicious recipe uses a chicken breast as a base covered in pizza toppings. Make any style of pizza you desire, but this pepperoni one is my favorite.

**NUTRITION PER 2 FILLET PIZZAS:**

**380** CALORIES
**20g** TOTAL FAT
**3g** NET CARBS
**40g** PROTEIN
**1g** DIETARY FIBER

PREP TIME
**5 mins**

COOK TIME
**15 mins**

MAKES
**6 fillet pizzas**

SERVING SIZE
**2 fillet pizzas**

3 medium skinless chicken breasts (12oz [340g])

½ cup passata sauce (seedless tomato purée)

1 tsp garlic powder

½ tsp dried parsley

½ tsp dried basil

¼ tsp sea salt

½ tsp ground black pepper

12 slices of pepperoni

½ cup grated mozzarella cheese

**1.** Set the air fryer temp to 350°F (175°C).

**2.** Place the chicken in the fryer basket and cook until lightly cooked and opaque, about 5 minutes.

**3.** Remove the chicken from the fryer basket and slice the chicken horizontally to divide each breast in half to form fillets.

**4.** In a small bowl, combine the passata sauce, garlic powder, parsley, basil, salt, and pepper. Spoon this mixture over the cooked side of each chicken fillet. Top each fillet with 2 pepperoni slices and an equal amount of mozzarella.

**5.** Working in batches, place 3 fillets in the fryer basket, leaving ample room for hot air to circulate. Cook until the cheese has melted and the pepperoni becomes slightly crispy, about 5 minutes.

**6.** Transfer the fillet pizzas to a platter and serve immediately.

 **Tips** Get creative with different toppings or attempt to make your favorite style of pizza using the chicken and tomato base as a starter. Store the cooked fillet pizzas in an airtight container in the fridge for up to 4 days or in the freezer for up to 1 month.

# Creamy Tomato Meatballs

Meatballs often contain wheat breadcrumbs. But you can use just an egg and fragrant herbs to make awesome, easy meatballs while still staying keto.

**NUTRITION PER 3 MEATBALLS + ⅛ CUP SAUCE:**

**330** CALORIES
**24g** TOTAL FAT
**3g** NET CARBS
**25g** PROTEIN
**1g** DIETARY FIBER

PREP TIME
**5 mins**

COOK TIME
**25 mins**

MAKES
**12 meatballs**

SERVING SIZE
**3 meatballs + ⅛ cup sauce**

1lb (450g) ground beef (80% lean)

1 large egg

1 tsp sea salt

1 tsp ground black pepper

1 tsp garlic powder

1½ tsp dried oregano, divided

⅔ cup passata sauce (seedless tomato purée)

¼ cup heavy whipping cream, plus more

2 tbsp red wine

½ tsp dried parsley

½ tsp dried basil

fresh basil leaves (optional)

**1.** In a medium bowl, combine the ground beef, egg, salt, pepper, garlic powder, and 1 teaspoon of dried oregano. Mix well. Use a tablespoon to make 12 round meatballs. Place the meatballs on a plate, cover, and refrigerate for 20 minutes.

**2.** Set the air fryer temp to 350°F (175°C).

**3.** In a medium bowl, combine the passata sauce, whipping cream, red wine, parsley, basil, and the remaining ½ teaspoon of oregano.

**4.** Place the meatballs evenly around the bottom of a high-sided 8.5-inch (22cm) baking pan. Pour the passata mixture over the top.

**5.** Place the pan in the fryer basket and cook until the meatballs are dark brown on the outside and firm, about 25 minutes.

**6.** Transfer the meatballs to a platter. Drizzle more whipping cream and sprinkle fresh basil (if using) over the top. Serve immediately.

**Tips** Instead of using the multiple different dried herbs, you can easily substitute an Italian herb blend if your local grocery store has one. You can also omit the red wine without much change in flavor. Store the cooked meatballs in an airtight container in the fridge for up to 4 days or in the freezer for up to 1 month.

# Chicken Wings
## with Blue Cheese Sauce

Fried wings often use oils that can be inflammatory. This recipe uses healthy fats from avocado and full-fat dairy, plus a crispy protein coating cooked with air.

**NUTRITION PER 2 WINGS + 3 TABLESPOONS SAUCE:**

**545** CALORIES
**36g** TOTAL FAT
**2g** NET CARBS
**51g** PROTEIN
**1g** DIETARY FIBER

| PREP TIME | COOK TIME | MAKES | SERVING SIZE |
|---|---|---|---|
| **10 mins** | **25 mins** | **8 wings** | **2 wings + 3 tablespoons sauce** |

8 chicken wings (1lb [450g])

1 large egg

½ cup almond flour

2 tbsp unflavored whey protein powder

2 tsp celery salt

½ tsp garlic powder

¼ tsp sea salt

¼ tsp ground black pepper

**for the sauce**

1 tbsp crumbled blue cheese

2 tbsp full-fat sour cream

¼ cup full-fat Greek yogurt

2 tbsp avocado oil mayonnaise

½ tsp sea salt

½ tsp ground black pepper

1 tbsp chopped fresh parsley

**1.** Set the air fryer temp to 350°F (175°C). Spray the fryer basket with avocado oil.

**2.** Use paper towels to pat the chicken wings dry. Set aside.

**3.** In a small bowl, whisk the egg. In a large bowl, combine the almond flour, protein powder, celery salt, garlic powder, salt, and pepper. Dip each wing in the egg and then in the flour mixture.

**4.** Place the wings in the fryer basket, leaving ample room around each wing for air to circulate. Cook until the internal temperature reaches 165°F (75°C), about 25 minutes. (Cook the wings in batches if necessary.)

**5.** In a medium bowl, make the blue cheese sauce by combining the blue cheese, sour cream, yogurt, and mayonnaise. Add the salt, pepper, and parsley. Mix well. Place the sauce in a dipping bowl.

**6.** Transfer the wings to a platter. Serve immediately with the blue cheese sauce.

**Tips** This recipe works best with regular whey protein powder. If using a vegan protein powder, use half as much because the coating is much drier. You can also add a dash or two of hot sauce to the egg mixture. Separately store the cooked wings and the sauce in airtight containers in the fridge for up to 4 days. These wings are best eaten fresh.

# Garlic Parmesan Wings

Chicken wings are perfect for the air fryer and these are crispy and superbly coated in a cheesy garlic outer layer. Serve with a side salad for a main meal.

**NUTRITION PER 3 WINGS:**

**490** CALORIES
**37g** TOTAL FAT
**3g** NET CARBS
**33g** PROTEIN
**1g** DIETARY FIBER

PREP TIME
**5 mins**

COOK TIME
**20 mins**

MAKES
**6 wings**

SERVING SIZE
**3 wings**

1½ tsp garlic powder

2 tbsp olive oil

1 tsp sea salt

½ tsp ground black pepper

¼ cup grated Parmesan cheese

6 skin-on chicken wings (9oz [255g])

**1.** Set the air fryer temp to 350°F (175°C).

**2.** In a small bowl, combine the garlic powder, olive oil, salt, pepper, and Parmesan. Mix well. Use a brush or sprigs of fresh herbs to brush the olive oil mixture on both sides of the chicken wings.

**3.** Place the wings in the fryer basket and cook until they're crispy on the outside and they've reached an internal temperature of 165°F (75°C), about 20 minutes, flipping halfway through.

**4.** Transfer the wings to a wire rack for 5 minutes before serving.

 **Tips** Because some chicken wings are smaller or larger than others, make as much of the garlic and Parmesan coating as you need to cover your particular wings. Store the cooked wings in an airtight container for up to 4 days in the fridge or up to 1 month in the freezer.

# Pork Belly
## with Peppers & Peanuts

This combination of bell peppers, lime, peanuts, pork, garlic, and fennel will bring happiness to your kitchen and to the mouths of the people you're feeding.

**NUTRITION PER ½ CUP PORK BELLY + 1½ PEPPERS + 1 TABLESPOON PEANUTS:**

**460** CALORIES
**46g** TOTAL FAT
**5g** NET CARBS
**9g** PROTEIN
**1g** DIETARY FIBER

PREP TIME
**10 mins**

COOK TIME
**70 mins**

MAKES
**3 cups pork belly**

SERVING SIZE
**½ cup pork belly + 1½ peppers + 1 tablespoon of peanuts**

1lb (450g) pork belly

1 tsp fennel seeds

3 garlic cloves

1 tsp plus 3 tbsp sea salt

1 tsp ground black pepper

2 tbsp olive oil

9 mini bell peppers (various colors), cut into chunks

¼ cup chopped roasted peanuts

½ lime

**1.** In a large pot on the stovetop over medium heat, place the pork belly and cover with hot water. Bring to a steady boil for 25 minutes.

**2.** Remove the pork from the hot water and pat dry with paper towels. Place the pork skin side up on a large sheet of aluminum foil and cover the bottom and sides with the foil, leaving the top skin exposed. Refrigerate for 30 minutes to dry out the skin.

**3.** Set the air fryer temp to 400°F (200°C).

**4.** Use a mortar and pestle to grind together the fennel seeds, garlic, 1 teaspoon of salt, and pepper until the mixture forms a fine paste. Add the olive oil and stir.

**5.** Remove the foil from the pork. Use a pastry brush or a small bunch of herbs to brush the underside of the belly with the fennel mixture. Don't brush the skin.

**6.** Place the pork skin side up in the fryer basket and cover with the remaining 3 tablespoons of salt. Cook until the internal temperature reaches 165°F (75°C), about 40 minutes, checking every 15 minutes to ensure the top is starting to crackle.

**7.** Transfer the pork to a platter and remove the salt from the top. Cut the pork into bite-sized chunks and set aside. (Don't clean out the fryer basket. You'll use the leftover pork fat.)

**8.** Place the bell peppers and peanuts in the pork fat. Cook until the peppers are soft and the peanuts are crispy, about 5 minutes.

**9.** Transfer the peppers and peanuts to the platter. Serve immediately with the pork and a squeeze of lime juice.

**Tips** Store the entire meal in an airtight container in the fridge for up to 4 days or in the freezer for up to 1 month.

# Crispy Pork Belly

The best advantage of using an air fryer to cook pork belly is that it keeps the inside juicy while crisping the outer skin for crackling you've always dreamed of.

**NUTRITION PER ½ CUP PORK BELLY:**

**412** CALORIES
**42g** TOTAL FAT
**0g** NET CARBS
**7g** PROTEIN
**0g** DIETARY FIBER

PREP TIME
**10 mins**

COOK TIME
**70 mins**

MAKES
**3 cups pork belly**

SERVING SIZE
**½ cup pork belly**

1lb (450g) pork belly
1 tbsp olive oil
1 tsp Chinese five-spice powder
1 tsp plus 3 tbsp sea salt
1 tsp ground black pepper
5 garlic cloves, peeled

**1.** In a large pot on the stovetop over medium heat, place the pork belly and cover with hot water. Bring to a steady boil for 25 minutes.

**2.** Remove the pork from the hot water and pat dry with paper towels. Place the pork skin side up on a large sheet of aluminum foil. Cover the bottom and sides with the foil, leaving the top skin exposed. Refrigerate for 30 minutes to dry out the skin.

**3.** Set the air fryer temp to 400°F (200°C).

**4.** In a small bowl, combine the olive oil, Chinese five-spice powder, 1 teaspoon of salt, and pepper.

**5.** Remove the foil from the pork. Use a pastry brush or sprigs of herbs to brush the underside of the pork with the spice powder mixture. Don't brush the top.

**6.** Use a knife to make 5 small slashes on the underside and stuff each cut with a garlic clove. Return the pork to the aluminum foil, again leaving the top skin exposed.

**7.** Place the pork in the fryer basket and cover with the remaining 3 tablespoons of salt. Cook until the internal temperature reaches 165°F (75°C), about 40 minutes, checking every 15 minutes to ensure the top is starting to crackle.

**8.** Transfer the pork to a platter and remove the salt from the top. Cut the pork into bite-sized chunks. Serve immediately with your favorite sides.

 **Tips** Store the cooked pork belly in an airtight container in the fridge for up to 4 days or in the freezer for up to 1 month.

# Roasted Pork
## with Garlic & Fennel

Garlic and fennel are a time-tested match with roasted pork. The sweetness of fennel paired with the zest from garlic will make your mouth water.

NUTRITION PER
5oz (140g):

**420** CALORIES
**28g** TOTAL FAT
**0g** NET CARBS
**40g** PROTEIN
**1g** DIETARY FIBER

| PREP TIME | COOK TIME | MAKES | SERVING SIZE |
|---|---|---|---|
| **10 mins** | **60 mins** | **2lb (900g)** | **5oz (140g) with crackling** |

1 tsp fennel seeds

1 tsp plus 1 tbsp sea salt

1 tsp ground black pepper

3 garlic cloves

2 tbsp olive oil, divided

2lb (900g) boneless pork shoulder

**1.** Set the air fryer temp to 350°F (175°C).

**2.** Use a mortar and pestle to grind together the fennel seeds, 1 teaspoon of salt, and pepper. Use the salt to break up the fennel seeds until a fine paste forms. Add the garlic and continue to grind. Add 1 tablespoon of olive oil and mix with a spoon. Set aside.

**3.** Use a sharp knife to score the pork skin in a crosshatched pattern every ½ inch (1.25cm). Use paper towels to dry the skin as much as possible. Brush the underside of the pork with the fennel and garlic seasoning, but don't brush the skin.

**4.** Turn the pork back over so the skin side faces upward. Rub the skin with the remaining 1 tablespoon of olive oil and the remaining 1 tablespoon of salt.

**5.** Place the pork in the fryer basket and roast until the internal temperature reaches 170°F (80°C), about 50 minutes.

**6.** Raise the air fryer temp to 400°F (200°C). Cook the roast until the skin crisps up completely, about 10 minutes more.

**7.** Transfer the pork to a platter and allow to cool for 10 minutes. Slice into 1-inch (2.5cm) slices before serving.

 **Tips** Check the pork every 10 to 15 minutes to ensure the top is starting to crackle. Store the roasted pork in an airtight container in the fridge for up to 4 days or in the freezer for up to 1 month.

# Garlic Butter Steak

This combination of garlic, butter, and Worcestershire sauce is just begging to be paired with steak and will undoubtedly become a staple in your household.

**NUTRITION PER 1 STEAK + ½ COMPOUND BUTTER:**

**430** CALORIES
**36g** TOTAL FAT
**1g** NET CARBS
**28g** PROTEIN
**0g** DIETARY FIBER

PREP TIME
**5 mins**

COOK TIME
**7 to 10 mins**

MAKES
**2 steaks**

SERVING SIZE
**1 steak + ½ the compound butter**

3oz (90g) salted butter, softened

1 tbsp chopped fresh parsley

1 garlic clove, minced

½ tsp Worcestershire sauce

1 tsp sea salt, divided

2 sirloin strip steaks (7oz [200g])

½ tsp ground black pepper

1 tbsp olive oil

**1.** In a medium bowl, combine the butter, parsley, garlic, Worcestershire sauce, and ½ teaspoon of salt. Mix well. Place the garlic butter mixture into a small section of plastic wrap and roll into a small log. Freeze for 20 minutes.

**2.** Set the air fryer temp to 350°F (175°C).

**3.** Season the steaks with pepper and the remaining ½ teaspoon of salt. Rub the steaks with the olive oil.

**4.** Place the steaks in the fryer basket and cook until the fat has rendered and the outsides are brown, about 6½ minutes for medium and 10 minutes for well done.

**5.** Transfer the steaks to a platter and allow to cool for 5 minutes. Slice the steaks and the garlic butter. Top each steak with half the garlic butter before serving.

**Tips** Because air fryers have varying degrees of power, follow the guidelines in your air fryer's manual for cooking steak to the particular level of doneness you desire (rare, medium rare, etc.) (The air fryer used for this recipe is 1750W [very powerful].)

# Garlic & Ginger Beef Spare Ribs

Spare ribs are a fantastic cut of beef to marinate in garlic and ginger. This creates an Asian-inspired beef rib taste that's perfect for the ketogenic diet.

**NUTRITION PER 1 SPARE RIB:**

**625** CALORIES
**56g** TOTAL FAT
**1g** NET CARBS
**28g** PROTEIN
**1g** DIETARY FIBER

PREP TIME
**10 mins**

COOK TIME
**20 mins**

MAKES
**4 ribs**

SERVING SIZE
**1 spare rib**

1 tbsp tamari (or gluten-free soy sauce)

1 tbsp rice vinegar

1 tsp ground ginger

3 large garlic cloves, minced

½ tsp Chinese five-spice blend

1 tsp sea salt

½ tsp ground black pepper

4 large spare ribs (2lb [1kg])

**1.** In a large bowl, combine the tamari, rice vinegar, ginger, garlic, Chinese five-spice blend, salt, and pepper. Mix well.

**2.** Place the spare ribs in the bowl and coat generously with the marinade. Cover and refrigerate for 60 minutes.

**3.** Set the air fryer temp to 350°F (175°C).

**4.** Place the spare ribs meat side up in the fryer basket. Use a pastry brush or sprigs of fresh herbs to marinade the meat. Cook until the internal temperature reaches 170°F (80°C), about 20 minutes.

**5.** Transfer the spare ribs to a platter. Serve immediately with your favorite sides.

**Tips** If the beef ribs are a little too rare for your liking closer to the bone, I suggest using a sharp knife to remove the beef from the bone and cook that in the air fryer for 5 minutes more or until your preferred level of doneness is achieved. Store the cooked ribs in an airtight container in the fridge for up to 4 days or in the freezer for up to 1 month.

# Beef Curry

Make any weeknight meal feel like takeout perfection with this simple, delightful beef curry dish. This recipe features marinated beef cooked in a coconut sauce.

**NUTRITION PER ¾ CUP:**

**440** CALORIES
**36g** TOTAL FAT
**6g** NET CARBS
**23g** PROTEIN
**3g** DIETARY FIBER

PREP TIME
**10 mins**

COOK TIME
**15 mins**

MAKES
**3 cups**

SERVING SIZE
**¾ cup**

10oz (285g) chuck or blade steak, cubed

1 tbsp extra virgin olive oil

1 tsp sea salt

1 tsp ground black pepper

2 garlic cloves, crushed

1 tbsp minced ginger

1 tbsp tamari (or gluten-free soy sauce)

1 tbsp curry powder

½ white or brown onion, diced

½ head of broccoli, cut into florets

1 cup coconut cream

**1.** In a medium bowl, combine the beef, olive oil, salt, pepper, garlic, ginger, tamari, and curry powder. Toss to coat evenly. Cover and refrigerate for 60 minutes to marinate.

**2.** Set the air fryer temp to 350°F (175°C).

**3.** Place the beef, marinade, and onion in a high-sided baking dish. Place the dish in the fryer basket and cook for 5 minutes.

**4.** Remove the dish from the fryer basket and add the broccoli and coconut cream. Stir to incorporate the cream.

**5.** Place the dish back in the fryer basket and cook for 10 minutes more or until the meat is cooked to your liking. (Ensure an internal temperature of at least 165°F [75°C].)

**6.** Remove the dish from the fryer basket. Serve the beef immediately with a side of Fried Cauliflower "Rice" (page 100).

 **Tips** This recipe is perfect for meal prep, so dividing the food into meal prep containers with some cauliflower rice can help you stay consistent during the week. Store the cooked beef in an airtight container in the fridge for up to 4 days or in the freezer for up to 1 month.

# Beef Skewers

Balsamic vinegar and Worcestershire sauce make a simple, tangy keto-friendly marinade that will give you succulent beef bites time and time again.

**NUTRITION PER 2 SKEWERS:**

**500** CALORIES
**36g** TOTAL FAT
**3g** NET CARBS
**40g** PROTEIN
**1g** DIETARY FIBER

PREP TIME
**10 mins**

COOK TIME
**10 mins**

MAKES
**4 skewers**

SERVING SIZE
**2 skewers**

10oz (285g) sirloin steak, cut into 1-inch (2.5cm) cubes

2 tbsp olive oil

1 tbsp Worcestershire sauce

¼ tsp sea salt

¼ tsp ground black pepper

1 tsp balsamic vinegar

½ red onion, cubed

**1.** In a medium bowl, combine the beef, olive oil, Worcestershire sauce, salt, pepper, and balsamic vinegar. Mix well. Cover and refrigerate for 30 minutes.

**2.** Set the air fryer temp to 350°F (175°C).

**3.** Alternate threading an equal amount of steak and onion on 4 skewers. (Reserve the marinade.)

**4.** Place the skewers in the fryer basket and cook until the beef starts to brown, about 5 minutes. Brush both sides of the skewers with the reserved marinade and then flip. Cook until completely browned, about 5 minutes more.

**5.** Transfer the skewers from the air fryer and serve immediately.

**Tips** If you're using bamboo skewers, soak them in water for 30 minutes while your beef is marinating so they don't burn. Store the cooked skewers in an airtight container in the fridge for up to 4 days or in the freezer for up to 1 month.

# Beef Casserole
## with Bacon & Walnuts

Bacon and walnuts are a winning flavor combination to bring this beef casserole to life. Mushrooms and broccoli make for great additions to this steak dish.

**NUTRITION PER 1 CUP:**

**445** CALORIES
**33g** TOTAL FAT
**5g** NET CARBS
**32g** PROTEIN
**2g** DIETARY FIBER

PREP TIME
**10 mins**

COOK TIME
**15 mins**

MAKES
**4 cups**

SERVING SIZE
**1 cup**

7oz (200g) chuck or blade steak, cubed

1 tbsp freshly squeezed lime juice

1 tsp sea salt

1 tsp ground black pepper

½ cup chopped walnuts

5oz (140g) bacon (7 to 10 slices), diced

2 cups button mushrooms, sliced

½ head of broccoli, cut into florets

1 tbsp extra virgin olive oil

1 vegetable stock cube, crushed

1 cup water

1½ tsp gelatin powder

**1.** In a medium bowl, combine the beef, lime juice, salt, and pepper. Toss to coat evenly. Cover and refrigerate for 60 minutes to marinate.

**2.** Set the air fryer temp to 350°F (175°C).

**3.** Place the walnuts in the fryer basket and toast until crispy, about 4 minutes. Remove the walnuts from the fryer basket and set aside.

**4.** In a high-sided baking dish, combine the beef, marinade, bacon, mushrooms, broccoli, olive oil, and vegetable stock cube.

**5.** Place the dish in the fryer basket and cook until the beef has browned and the mushrooms are well cooked, about 10 minutes.

**6.** Remove the dish from the fryer basket and add the water and gelatin powder. Thoroughly mix in the powder with a spoon.

**7.** Return the dish to the fryer basket and cook until slightly thickened, about 5 minutes more.

**8.** Remove the dish from the fryer basket and sprinkle the walnuts over the top. Serve immediately with your favorite vegetables.

 **Tips** Gelatin powder gives the sauce a creamy, thicker, gravy-type consistency, but you can replace it by adding 2 egg yolks right at the end while the dish is still hot. Egg yolks have lecithin, which helps emulsify and thicken sauces. Store the cooked casserole in an airtight container in the fridge for up to 4 days or in the freezer for up to 1 month.

# Crispy Chicken Thighs
## with Lemon & Rosemary

Chicken thighs infused with zest from a lemon and the aromatics of rosemary make a simple dinner for two or you can double the recipe for a family meal.

**NUTRITION PER 1 THIGH:**

**300** CALORIES
**20g** TOTAL FAT
**1g** NET CARBS
**28g** PROTEIN
**0g** DIETARY FIBER

PREP TIME
**5 mins**

COOK TIME
**16 mins**

MAKES
**2 thighs**

SERVING SIZE
**1 thigh**

1 tbsp olive oil

1 tbsp freshly squeezed lemon juice

1 tsp dried rosemary

½ tsp sea salt

½ tsp ground black pepper

2 large boneless, skin-on chicken thighs (7oz [200g])

**1.** In a medium bowl, combine the olive oil, lemon juice, rosemary, salt, and pepper.

**2.** Place the chicken in the bowl and cover with the marinade. Mix well to coat. Cover and refrigerate for 30 minutes.

**3.** Set the air fryer temp to 400°F (200°C).

**4.** Remove the thighs from the fridge and reserve the marinade. Place the thighs skin side up in the fryer basket and cook for 4 minutes. Brush each thigh along the top of the skin with the reserved marinade. Repeat this every 4 minutes until 16 minutes total have elapsed. The chicken will have a crispy skin and the internal temperature should be 165°F (75°C) or above.

**5.** Transfer the thighs to a platter and serve immediately.

 **Tips** Using a pastry brush to brush the chicken is best, but you can also use a large rosemary sprig. If your chicken thighs are bone-in, then remove the meat from the bone before marinating. Store the cooked chicken in an airtight container in the fridge for up to 4 days or in the freezer for up to 1 month.

# Stuffed Mushrooms

These cheesy stuffed mushrooms are packed with protein. They make an appetizing snack or they can be a main meal when combined with a side salad.

**NUTRITION PER 1 MUSHROOM:**

**100** CALORIES
**7g** TOTAL FAT
**4g** NET CARBS
**7g** PROTEIN
**1g** DIETARY FIBER

PREP TIME
**5 mins**

COOK TIME
**5 mins**

MAKES
**5 mushrooms**

SERVING SIZE
**1 mushroom**

3oz (90g) feta cheese, crumbled

2 tbsp sour cream

2 garlic cloves, crushed

1 tsp dried parsley

¼ tsp sea salt

1 tsp ground black pepper

5 large portobello mushrooms (14oz [400g]), cleaned, stems and gills removed

2oz (60g) shredded mozzarella cheese

**1.** Set the air fryer temp to 350°F (175°C).

**2.** In a medium bowl, combine the feta, sour cream, garlic, parsley, salt, and pepper. Mix well. Spoon an equal amount into each mushroom and top each with an equal amount of mozzarella.

**3.** Place the mushrooms in the fryer basket and cook until they begin to turn color and become slightly soft, about 5 minutes.

**4.** Transfer the mushrooms to a platter and serve immediately.

 **Tips** Simply brushing the tops of each mushroom with a clean paper towel will be enough to clean them. Try not to wash the mushrooms because they'll become waterlogged and soggy once cooked. Store the cooked mushrooms in an airtight container lined with a paper towel in the fridge for up to 4 days.

# Mediterranean Halloumi Bake

Halloumi cheese is made from goat and sheep milk. In this recipe, fresh tomatoes and an array of spices give this dish a Mediterranean feel you dream about.

**NUTRITION PER 1 CUP:**

**420** CALORIES
**36g** TOTAL FAT
**5g** NET CARBS
**20g** PROTEIN
**2g** DIETARY FIBER

PREP TIME
**5 mins**

COOK TIME
**13 mins**

MAKES
**2 cups**

SERVING SIZE
**1 cup**

4 large tomatoes (7oz [200g]), diced

6 kalamata olives, thinly sliced

2 garlic cloves, minced

1 tbsp olive oil

1 tsp dried oregano

1 tsp dried parsley

½ tsp sea salt

½ tsp ground black pepper

7oz (200g) halloumi cheese, sliced into 12 strips

½ lemon

**1.** Set the air fryer temp to 400°F (200°C).

**2.** In a baking dish, combine the tomatoes, olives, garlic, olive oil, oregano, parsley, salt, and pepper. Mix well.

**3.** Place the dish in the fryer basket and cook until the tomatoes become soft and the herbs are fragrant, about 5 minutes.

**4.** Remove the dish from the fryer basket and top the tomato mixture with the halloumi.

**5.** Return the dish to the fryer basket and cook until the halloumi has browned on top, about 7 minutes more.

**6.** Remove the dish from the fryer basket and squeeze the lemon over the top before serving.

 **Tips** Any dried or fresh Mediterranean herbs will work in this recipe, such as basil, cilantro (coriander), cumin, dill, mint, paprika, rosemary, sumac, or thyme. Use your favorite keto-friendly bread to soak up the sauce. Store the cooked halloumi bake in an airtight container in the fridge for up to 5 days or in the freezer for up to 1 month.

# Salty & Spicy Tofu

Air-fried tofu becomes firm and almost like cheese.
This recipe's flavor combo will make you want more.
Enjoy this dish with a creamy dip if cayenne is too hot.

**NUTRITION PER
7 STRIPS:**

**80** CALORIES
**3g** TOTAL FAT
**4g** NET CARBS
**8g** PROTEIN
**2g** DIETARY FIBER

PREP TIME
**10 mins**

COOK TIME
**40 mins**

MAKES
**28 strips**

SERVING SIZE
**7 strips**

1lb (450g) extra-firm tofu

1 tsp ground paprika

1 tsp ground cayenne pepper

2 tbsp sea salt

2 tbsp ground black pepper

**1.** Cut the tofu into 28 strips, each about 1 inch (2.5cm) long. Place the tofu on 4 paper towels. Place 4 more paper towels over the tofu and place a plate on top to help squeeze the water from the tofu. Let the tofu sit until enough water has drained from the tofu and the paper towels are sufficiently soaked, about 20 minutes.

**2.** Set the air fryer temp to 400°F (200°C).

**3.** In a medium bowl, combine the tofu, paprika, cayenne, salt, and pepper. Toss well to coat.

**4.** Working in batches, place 14 strips of tofu in the fryer basket and cook until cooked through, about 20 minutes, turning the tofu every 5 minutes to brown each side.

**5.** Transfer the tofu to a platter and serve immediately.

 **Tips** Feel free to get creative with herbs and spices of your choice, such as salt and vinegar, smoked paprika, or even lemon and basil. Store the cooked tofu in an airtight container lined with a paper towel in the fridge for up to 7 days or in the freezer for up to 1 month.

# Breaded Fish

Almond flour and whey protein powder—with a hint of paprika—create a crunchy outer coating for fish. Pair this dish with a dry white wine.

**NUTRITION PER 5oz (140g):**

**346** CALORIES
**17g** TOTAL FAT
**3g** NET CARBS
**44g** PROTEIN
**3g** DIETARY FIBER

PREP TIME
**10 mins**

COOK TIME
**30 mins**

MAKES
**10oz (285g)**

SERVING SIZE
**5oz (140g)**

1 large egg

½ cup almond flour

2 tbsp unflavored whey protein powder

¼ tsp paprika

¼ tsp dried dill

½ tsp garlic powder

¼ tsp sea salt

¼ tsp ground black pepper

9oz (255g) boneless fish fillets (cod, flake, or basa)

½ lemon

**1.** Set the air fryer temp to 360°F (180°C). Spray the fryer basket with nonstick cooking spray.

**2.** In a small bowl, whisk the egg. In a medium bowl, combine the almond flour, protein powder, paprika, dill, garlic powder, salt, and pepper.

**3.** Pat the fish dry with paper towels. Dip the fish in the egg and then in the flour mixture. Ensure the fish is well coated.

**4.** Working in batches, place half the fish in the fryer basket and cook until lightly golden on the outside, about 15 minutes, flipping halfway through.

**5.** Remove the fish from the fryer basket and allow to cool for 2 minutes. Squeeze a little lemon juice over the fish before serving.

**Tips** Make a quick aioli in a small bowl by combining 3 tablespoons of mayonnaise, 1 teaspoon of minced garlic, and 1 teaspoon of Dijon mustard. Store the cooked fish in an airtight container in the fridge for up to 2 days.

# Lamb Larb

Larb is a spicy Thai meat salad that's usually wrapped in a large lettuce leaf. While larb is generally made with pork, my version uses lamb.

**NUTRITION PER 2 LETTUCE LEAVES + ½ CUP LARB:**

**400** CALORIES
**30g** TOTAL FAT
**4g** NET CARBS
**27g** PROTEIN
**1g** DIETARY FIBER

| PREP TIME | COOK TIME | MAKES | SERVING SIZE |
|---|---|---|---|
| **15 mins** | **17 mins** | **2 cups** | **2 lettuce leaves + ½ cup larb** |

1lb (450g) ground lamb

4 garlic cloves, minced

4 green onions, sliced

2 hot chili peppers (remove seeds for mild), chopped

½ bunch of cilantro (coriander), chopped

3 tbsp freshly squeezed lime juice

1 tbsp fish sauce

2 tbsp sesame seed oil

¼ tsp sea salt

¼ tsp ground black pepper

8 large lettuce leaves

**1.** Set the air fryer temp to 360°F (180°C).

**2.** Place the lamb on a baking pan. Place the pan in the fryer basket and cook until some brown color begins to form, about 10 minutes, stirring every 3 minutes.

**3.** In a small blender or food processor, combine the garlic, green onions, chili peppers, and cilantro. Pulse until chunky.

**4.** Add the blended ingredients, lime juice, and fish sauce to the lamb. Cook until the lamb is sufficiently cooked and some nice color develops, about 7 minutes more.

**5.** Remove the pan from the fryer basket and season the lamb with the sesame seed oil, salt, and pepper. Mix well and allow to cool for 5 minutes. Serve the lamb in large lettuce leaves.

 **Tips** You can use chicken, pork, turkey, or beef instead. The taste doesn't change too dramatically because the majority of the flavor comes from the herbs and spices. Store the cooked lamb in an airtight container in the fridge for up to 4 days or in the freezer for up to 1 month.

# Salmon Patties

This dish is easy to make, tastes fresh and delicious, and is a versatile main meal. Pair with a creamy side or even as the patty for a keto-friendly burger.

**NUTRITION PER 3 PATTIES:**
**210** CALORIES
**11g** TOTAL FAT
**3g** NET CARBS
**26g** PROTEIN
**3g** DIETARY FIBER

PREP TIME
**5 mins**

COOK TIME
**20 mins**

MAKES
**12 patties**

SERVING SIZE
**3 patties**

14oz (400g) skinless salmon
½ red bell pepper, chopped
¼ red onion, chopped
¼ cup chopped fresh parsley
1 tsp sea salt
1 tsp ground black pepper
⅓ cup coconut flour
1 large egg
1 tbsp olive oil
1 tbsp tamari (or gluten-free soy sauce)
juice of ½ lime

**1.** In a food processor, combine the ingredients. Blend on high until well combined and no lumps are present.

**2.** Use a spoon a little larger than a tablespoon to make 12 portions. Flatten these portions into patties with your hands and place them on a plate. Cover and refrigerate for 30 minutes.

**3.** Set the air fryer temp to 350°F (175°C). Spray the fryer basket with olive oil.

**4.** Working in batches, place 6 patties on a baking pan and place the pan in the fryer basket. Cook until brown on the outside and firm to touch, about 10 minutes, flipping halfway through.

**5.** Transfer the patties to a platter and allow to cool for 5 minutes before serving.

**Tips** If you don't have a food processor, finely chop all the ingredients and mix them together in a large bowl. The mixture might not come together as easily, but the time spent in the fridge will help bind the ingredients. Store the cooked salmon patties in an airtight container in the fridge for up to 4 days or in the freezer for up to 1 month.

# Smoky Chicken Pizza

Keto pizza is often made with a mozzarella base. This recipe uses chicken as the base—and it tastes amazing. You can also easily make this dairy-free.

**NUTRITION PER 2 SLICES:**

**325** CALORIES
**20g** TOTAL FAT
**2g** NET CARBS
**33g** PROTEIN
**1g** DIETARY FIBER

PREP TIME
**10 mins**

COOK TIME
**13 mins**

MAKES
**8 slices**

SERVING SIZE
**2 slices**

10oz (285g) skinless chicken breast, diced

¼ cup grated Parmesan cheese

1 tbsp olive oil

1 tsp dried parsley

1 tsp dried oregano

½ tsp sea salt

½ tsp ground black pepper

2 tbsp passata sauce (seedless tomato purée)

1 tsp smoked paprika

2oz (60g) bacon, diced

1oz (30g) sliced salami

2oz (60g) grated mozzarella cheese

**1.** Set the air fryer temp to 400°F (200°C).

**2.** In a food processor, combine the chicken, Parmesan, olive oil, parsley, oregano, salt, and pepper. Process until well combined.

**3.** Place the chicken mixture into a 8.5-inch (22cm) round pizza pan and press flat, leaving a crust-sized edge around the outside.

**4.** Place the pan in the fryer basket and cook until slightly golden brown on the edges, about 7 minutes. Remove the pan from the fryer basket.

**5.** In a small bowl, combine the passata sauce and paprika. Spread this over the chicken. Top with the bacon, salami, and mozzarella.

**6.** Return the pan to the fryer basket and cook until the cheese has melted and the bacon and salami are crispy, about 5 minutes more.

**7.** Remove the pan from the fryer basket and slice the pizza into 8 slices before serving.

**Tips** Store the baked pizza in an airtight container in the fridge for up to 4 days or in the freezer for up to 1 month. Store the uncooked base with uncooked toppings in an airtight container in the freezer for up to 1 month. Place the pizza in the air fryer at 400°F (200°C) for 10 minutes to cook from frozen.

# Sides

# Breaded Onion Rings

Onion rings are a classic deep-fried snack. This recipe turns them low-carb by using a few key ingredients and makes them more healthy by using an air fryer.

PREP TIME
**5 mins**

COOK TIME
**4 mins**

MAKES
**8 rings**

SERVING SIZE
**8 rings**

1 large egg

1oz (30g) unflavored whey protein powder

½ tsp sea salt

½ tsp ground black pepper

1 tsp dried parsley

½ large white onion, sliced into 8 rings

**1.** Set the air fryer temp to 350°F (175°C). Spray the fryer basket with nonstick cooking spray.

**2.** In a small bowl, whisk the egg. In a separate small bowl, combine the protein powder, salt, pepper, and parsley.

**3.** Dip each onion ring in the egg and then in the protein powder mixture to coat the outside.

**4.** Place the onion rings in the fryer basket and ensure ample room for air to circulate around the edges. Cook for 4 minutes or until the onion rings reach your desired level of crispiness.

**5.** Transfer the onion rings to a platter and serve immediately.

 **Tips** Whey protein powder is essential to getting a dry, crispy exterior to these onion rings. Unflavored whey protein can be purchased from your local health food store or online in bulk. Whey protein isolate is lowest in carbs. Store the cooked rings in an airtight container in the fridge for up to 4 days. I wouldn't recommend freezing the cooked rings, but you can store the uncooked rings in an airtight container in the freezer for up to 1 month.

# Breaded Cheese Bites

For all you cheese lovers, these bites are an indulgent way to love cheese the right way using your air fryer: crispy on the outside and gooey on the inside.

**NUTRITION PER 3 BITES:**

**313** CALORIES
**26g** TOTAL FAT
**3g** NET CARBS
**17g** PROTEIN
**1g** DIETARY FIBER

PREP TIME
**10 mins**

COOK TIME
**8 mins**

MAKES
**12 bites**

SERVING SIZE
**3 bites**

2 large eggs, whisked, divided

2 cups grated mozzarella cheese

2 tbsp grated Parmesan cheese

½ tsp sea salt, divided

½ tsp ground black pepper, divided

¼ cup almond flour

1 tsp garlic powder

¼ tsp dried basil

2 tbsp olive oil

**1.** In a medium bowl, combine the mozzarella, Parmesan, 1 whisked egg, ¼ teaspoon of salt, and ¼ teaspoon of pepper. Mix well.

**2.** Roll the mixture into 12 balls, each about 1 tablespoon in size. Place the balls on a plate and freeze for 30 minutes.

**3.** Set the air fryer temp to 400°F (200°C). Spray the fryer basket with nonstick cooking spray.

**4.** In a medium bowl, combine the almond flour, garlic powder, basil, the remaining ¼ teaspoon of salt, and the remaining ¼ teaspoon of pepper.

**5.** Remove the cheese balls from the freezer. Dip the balls in the remaining 1 whisked egg and then in the almond flour mixture.

**6.** Working in batches, place 6 balls in the fryer basket and brush each one with a little olive oil. Cook until slightly golden, about 4 minutes, flipping halfway through.

**7.** Remove the cheese bites from the fryer basket and allow to cool for 2 minutes before serving.

**Tip** Store the cooked bites in the fridge for up to 4 days or in the freezer for up to 1 month, although they're best frozen uncooked.

# Cauliflower Mac & Cheese

Nothing is more comforting than mac and cheese. This low-carb version uses cauliflower and includes bacon and a hint of Dijon mustard.

**NUTRITION PER 1½ CUPS:**

**650** CALORIES
**60g** TOTAL FAT
**8g** NET CARBS
**21g** PROTEIN
**3g** DIETARY FIBER

PREP TIME
**10 mins**

COOK TIME
**25 mins**

MAKES
**6 cups**

SERVING SIZE
**1½ cups**

4 slices of bacon

1 medium head of cauliflower

1 tbsp olive oil

6oz (170g) cream cheese, room temperature

1 cup heavy whipping cream

1 tsp Dijon mustard

1½ cups grated Colby cheese, divided

¼ tsp sea salt

¼ tsp ground black pepper

**1.** Set the air fryer temp to 360°F (180°C).

**2.** Place the bacon in the fryer basket and cook until crispy, about 5 minutes. Remove the bacon from the fryer basket. Dice the bacon and set aside.

**3.** Lower the air fryer temp to 320°F (160°C).

**4.** Cut the cauliflower into florets and then cut the florets in half. Place the florets and olive oil in a large bowl. Mix well to coat. Place the florets on a baking pan.

**5.** Place the pan in the fryer basket and cook until tender, about 13 minutes.

**6.** Place the cream cheese in a large bowl. Use a hand mixer to add the whipping cream a little at a time. Mix well. Add the Dijon mustard and 1 cup of Colby. Mix again.

**7.** Raise the air fryer temp to 360°F (180°C).

**8.** Pour the cheese mixture over the cooked cauliflower and cover with the remaining ½ cup of Colby. Cook until warm all the way through, about 5 minutes more.

**9.** Remove the pan from the fryer basket and sprinkle the bacon over the top. Season with salt and pepper before serving.

 **Tips** Garnish with green herbs or crunchy pistachio nuts for additional texture. Store the cooked mac and cheese in an airtight container in the fridge for up to 4 days or in the freezer for up to 1 month.

# Roasted "Potatoes"

Potatoes have too many carbs for a strict keto diet, but you'll be surprised by how roasted radishes are similar in look and taste to a good old roasted potato.

**NUTRITION PER ½ CUP:**

**125** CALORIES
**14g** TOTAL FAT
**1g** NET CARBS
**1g** PROTEIN
**1g** DIETARY FIBER

PREP TIME
**5 mins**

COOK TIME
**18 mins**

MAKES
**1 cup**

SERVING SIZE
**½ cup**

7 large radishes, leaves trimmed

2 tbsp olive oil

½ tsp sea salt

¼ tsp ground black pepper

1 large sprig of rosemary

**1.** Set the air fryer temp to 360°F (180°C).

**2.** Quarter the radishes into wedges. In a medium bowl, combine the radishes, olive oil, salt, and pepper. Mix well. Place the radishes and rosemary on a baking pan.

**3.** Place the pan in the fryer basket and cook until the skins begin to turn crispy and the insides are soft, about 18 minutes. The radishes are done when fork tender.

**4.** Remove the pan from the fryer basket and discard the rosemary before serving.

**Tips** Get creative with the herbs you add to these roasted radishes. Thyme, parsley, oregano, or basil are all great. Mint or chives can also offer a wonderful flavor addition. Store the cooked radishes in an airtight container in the fridge for up to 4 days, but they're best served fresh.

# Rosemary & Garlic Mushrooms

This recipe is a favorite in my household. We serve it with steak or even fried eggs. You'll delight in how well the mushrooms absorb the rosemary flavor.

**NUTRITION PER ½ CUP:**

**180** CALORIES
**18g** TOTAL FAT
**3g** NET CARBS
**4g** PROTEIN
**2g** DIETARY FIBER

PREP TIME
**5 mins**

COOK TIME
**7 mins**

MAKES
**1 cup**

SERVING SIZE
**½ cup**

7oz (200g) button mushrooms (about 20), stems removed
3 tbsp salted butter
1 large sprig of fresh rosemary
2 garlic cloves, minced
½ tsp sea salt
½ tsp ground black pepper

**1.** Set the air fryer temp to 400°F (200°C).

**2.** Cut the mushrooms into thirds and place in a shallow baking dish. Add the butter, rosemary, garlic, salt, and pepper.

**3.** Place the dish in the fryer basket and cook until the mushrooms have wilted and absorbed a lot of the butter, about 6½ minutes, stirring every 2 minutes to ensure the mushrooms absorb the butter.

**4.** Transfer the mushrooms to a platter and discard the rosemary before serving.

 **Tips** Keeping the rosemary on the stem as much as possible will help you remove it at the end, but if you don't mind the texture of chopped fresh rosemary, chop the leaves and mix with the mushrooms. Store the cooked mushrooms in an airtight container in the fridge for up to 4 days.

# Roasted Balsamic Mixed Vegetables

This mix of autumn-warming vegetables coated in a zesty balsamic marinade gives depth to an otherwise ordinary array of side vegetables.

**NUTRITION PER ⅓ CUP:**

**130** CALORIES
**11g** TOTAL FAT
**5g** NET CARBS
**2g** PROTEIN
**3g** DIETARY FIBER

PREP TIME
**10 mins**

COOK TIME
**12 mins**

MAKES
**1⅓ cups**

SERVING SIZE
**⅓ cup**

½ red onion, chopped

½ large head of broccoli, cut into small florets

1 medium red bell pepper, chopped

1 tbsp balsamic vinegar

1 tsp Dijon mustard

3 tbsp olive oil

1 garlic clove, minced

1 tbsp chopped fresh rosemary

¼ tsp sea salt

¼ tsp ground black pepper

½ lemon

**1.** Set the air fryer temp to 360°F (180°C).

**2.** In a large bowl, combine the red onion, broccoli, and bell pepper. In a small bowl, combine the balsamic vinegar, Dijon mustard, olive oil, garlic, rosemary, salt, and pepper. Pour this mixture over the vegetables and mix well to coat.

**3.** Place the vegetables in the fryer basket and roast until the broccoli is dark but not burnt, about 12 minutes, mixing halfway through to ensure even browning on all sides.

**4.** Remove the vegetables from the fryer basket and squeeze a little lemon juice over the top before serving.

**Tips** The spices and herbs used for these vegetables make a versatile marinade and can be used for beef skewers or chicken pieces. Store the roasted vegetables in an airtight container in the fridge for up to 4 days.

# Brussels Sprout Chips

Chips made from Brussels sprouts are the ultimate side dish. Covered in salt, these cruciferous bites are the ideal vegetable to eat for a healthy lifestyle.

**NUTRITION PER ½ CUP:**

**155** CALORIES
**14g** TOTAL FAT
**5g** NET CARBS
**3g** PROTEIN
**3g** DIETARY FIBER

PREP TIME
**10 mins**

COOK TIME
**5 mins**

MAKES
**1 cup**

SERVING SIZE
**½ cup**

8 Brussels sprouts (3oz [90g])
2 tbsp coconut oil, melted
½ tsp salt
½ tsp dried thyme
½ lemon

**1.** Set the air fryer temp to 360°F (180°C).

**2.** Cut the Brussels sprouts in half and slice through the base at a 45-degree angle. This allows you to remove the layers of the sprouts so they resemble chips.

**3.** In a large bowl, combine the sprouts, coconut oil, salt, and thyme. Mix well.

**4.** Place the sprouts in the fryer basket and cook until the chips are crispy and cooked through, about 5 minutes.

**5.** Transfer the chips to a plate and squeeze a little lemon juice over the top before serving.

**Tips** Feel free to use any oil you prefer because not everyone enjoys cooking with coconut oil. Olive oil, ghee, and avocado oil are all fantastic substitutes and are just as healthy. Store the cooked chips in an airtight container in the fridge for up to 4 days.

# Asian-Style Broccolini
## with Pine Nuts

This side dish merges Broccolini and aromatic pine nuts covered in an Asian-style balsamic dressing. This dish pairs well with chicken or fish.

PREP TIME
**10 mins**

COOK TIME
**15 mins**

MAKES
**1 bunch**

SERVING SIZE
**½ bunch Broccolini + 2 tablespoons pine nuts**

¼ cup pine nuts

1 bunch of Broccolini (6oz [170g])

1 tbsp olive oil

1 tsp balsamic vinegar

1 tbsp rice vinegar

1 garlic clove, minced

¼ tsp sea salt

½ tsp ground black pepper

1 tsp sesame seed oil

½ lemon

**1.** Set the air fryer temp to 360°F (180°C).

**2.** Place the pine nuts on a baking pan. Place the pan in the fryer basket and toast until fragrant, about 3 minutes. Remove the pan from the fryer basket and set aside.

**3.** Cut off any overly woody ends from the Broccolini. Slice those woody sections into thin strips. In a large bowl, combine the Broccolini, olive oil, balsamic vinegar, rice vinegar, garlic, salt, and pepper. Mix well.

**4.** Place the Broccolini in the fryer basket and cook until the stems are soft and the florets are crispy, about 7 minutes, mixing halfway through to ensure the florets don't burn.

**5.** Remove the Broccolini from the fryer basket. Top with the roasted pine nuts and sesame seed oil. Squeeze a little lemon juice over the top before serving.

 **Tips** If you don't have rice vinegar, simply use half the amount of regular vinegar. Store the cooked Broccolini in an airtight container in the fridge for up to 4 days.

# Prosciutto-Wrapped Onion Rings

Prosciutto has the ideal thickness for hugging sweet onion and gets super crispy in the air fryer—a great midgame snack or fancy cheese board addition.

**NUTRITION PER 6 RINGS:**

**280** CALORIES
**25g** TOTAL FAT
**3g** NET CARBS
**12g** PROTEIN
**1g** DIETARY FIBER

PREP TIME
**10 mins**

COOK TIME
**6 mins**

MAKES
**12 rings**

SERVING SIZE
**6 rings**

½ medium yellow or brown onion

12 slices of prosciutto (4oz [120g])

3 tbsp olive oil

sea salt (optional)

¼ tsp ground black pepper

**1.** Set the air fryer temp to 400°F (200°C). Spray the fryer basket with nonstick cooking spray.

**2.** Slice the onion into 12 rings, about ½-inch (1.25cm) each. Wrap a prosciutto slice around each ring. Brush each prosciutto-wrapped onion with an equal amount of olive oil.

**3.** Working in batches, place 6 rings in the fryer basket and cook until the prosciutto becomes crispy, about 3 minutes, flipping halfway through.

**4.** Remove the rings from the fryer basket and allow to cool for 1 minute. Season with salt (if using) and pepper before serving.

 **Tip** These onion rings are best eaten fresh—they'll go soggy if stored in the fridge.

# Broccoli Florets
## with Romesco Sauce

Romesco is a tomato-based sauce with grilled peppers and crunchy nuts that's usually served with fish, but broccoli florets work even better.

**NUTRITION PER
1 BROCCOLI FLORET
+ ¼ CUP SAUCE:**

**228** CALORIES
**17g** TOTAL FAT
**10g** NET CARBS
**7g** PROTEIN
**6g** DIETARY FIBER

PREP TIME
**10 mins**

COOK TIME
**5 mins**

MAKES
**4 broccoli florets**

SERVING SIZE
**1 broccoli floret
+ ¼ cup sauce**

2 medium red bell peppers, quartered and seeds removed

¼ cup hazelnuts

¼ cup almonds

2 medium vine-ripened tomatoes, roughly chopped

1 hot chili pepper, seeds removed, diced

3 garlic cloves

2 tbsp coconut oil

1 sprig of rosemary, leaves only

1 tsp smoked paprika

2 tbsp apple cider vinegar

¼ cup olive oil

1 large head of broccoli, cut into 4 florets

¼ tsp sea salt

**1.** Set the air fryer temp to 360°F (180°C).

**2.** Place the bell peppers skin side up in the fryer basket and cook until the skins begin to blacken, about 15 minutes. Remove the peppers from the fryer basket and place in a medium bowl. Cover with an upside-down plate for 4 minutes to steam. Remove and discard the skins. Set the peppers aside.

**3.** Place the hazelnuts and almonds in the fryer basket and lightly toast for 5 minutes. Remove the hazelnuts and almonds from the fryer basket and set aside.

**4.** Place the tomatoes, chili pepper, garlic, coconut oil, rosemary, and paprika on a baking pan and mix to distribute the ingredients.

**5.** Place the pan in the fryer basket and cook until the tomatoes break down, about 10 minutes, stirring halfway through.

**6.** Remove the pan from the fryer basket and allow the tomatoes to cool for 3 minutes. Place the peppers, nuts, apple cider vinegar, olive oil, and tomato mixture in a food processor. Pulse until the mixture becomes chunky yet slightly smooth. Set aside.

**7.** Raise the air fryer temp to 400°F (200°C). Dip the tops of the broccoli florets in water.

**8.** Place the florets in the fryer basket and cook until crispy, about 10 minutes.

**9.** Spread ¼ cup of the sauce on a plate and transfer the florets onto the top of the sauce. Season with salt before serving.

**Tips** Add some spice to the sauce by adding the chili pepper seeds. Romesco goes well with eggs or any kind of protein (including fish). Store the cooked broccoli in an airtight container in the fridge for up to 3 days. Store leftover romesco in an airtight container in the fridge for up to 1 week or in the freezer for up to 1 month.

# Zucchini Fries

Zucchini fries can be tricky to get right using an oven, but thanks to the air fryer's powerful capabilities, these are super crispy, delicious, and craveable.

**NUTRITION PER 1 CUP:**

**120** CALORIES
**7g** TOTAL FAT
**5g** NET CARBS
**9g** PROTEIN
**2g** DIETARY FIBER

PREP TIME
**10 mins**

COOK TIME
**10 mins**

MAKES
**2 cups**

SERVING SIZE
**1 cup**

1 large zucchini

1 large egg

¼ cup grated Parmesan cheese

¼ tsp sea salt, plus more

¼ tsp ground black pepper, plus more

**1.** Set the air fryer temp to 400°F (200°C). Spray the fryer basket with nonstick cooking spray.

**2.** Cut the zucchini into 2½-inch-long (6.25cm) strips. Place these strips on a plate lined with paper towels and press over the top with additional paper towels to remove all the excess liquid from the zucchini. Try to get them as dry as possible.

**3.** In a small bowl, whisk the egg. In a separate small bowl, combine the Parmesan, salt, and pepper. Dip the zucchini in the egg and then in the Parmesan mixture. Ensure to coat evenly.

**4.** Working in batches, place half the zucchini strips in the fryer basket and cook until golden on the outside, about 5 minutes, flipping halfway through.

**5.** Remove the fries from the fryer basket and allow to cool for 2 minutes. Season with more salt and pepper before serving.

 **Tips** Pair this with a steak and a side salad or simply dip the fries in a sugar-free tomato sauce. These fries are best served fresh.

# Nut-Free Sesame Seed Bread

Some keto breads tend to use nuts. Many people are also allergic to nuts or avoid coconuts, so I've created a nut-free keto bread based on sesame seed flour.

**NUTRITION PER 1 SLICE:**

**354** CALORIES
**28g** TOTAL FAT
**1g** NET CARBS
**10g** PROTEIN
**4g** DIETARY FIBER

PREP TIME
**15 mins**

COOK TIME
**45 mins**

MAKES
**12 slices**

SERVING SIZE
**1 slice**

7 large eggs, room
 temperature

1¾ cups sesame seed flour

1 tsp baking powder

½ tsp sea salt

½ tsp xanthan gum

¼ cup olive oil

**1.** Set the air fryer temp to 360°F (180°C). Spray an 8-inch (20cm) square pan with nonstick cooking spray.

**2.** In a large bowl, combine the eggs, sesame seed flour, baking powder, and salt. Mix well.

**3.** Add the xanthan gum and olive oil. Stir thoroughly to ensure the mixture is well combined. Pour this mixture into the pan.

**4.** Place the pan in the fryer basket and bake for 45 minutes. Check for doneness by inserting a skewer in the middle. If the skewer comes out clean, the loaf is done.

**5.** Remove the loaf from the fryer basket and allow to cool for 10 minutes before slicing into 12 slices.

**Tips** If you can't find sesame seed flour, just pulse the same quantity of sesame seeds in a food processor until the mixture resembles flour. Store the baked bread in an airtight container in the fridge for up to 4 days or in the freezer for up to 2 months.

# Almond Flour Bread

This keto loaf uses eggs and almond flour to develop the bread-like texture, but you can replace the eggs with 2 cups of whey protein powder for less egginess.

**NUTRITION PER 1 SLICE:**

**354** CALORIES
**28g** TOTAL FAT
**1g** NET CARBS
**10g** PROTEIN
**4g** DIETARY FIBER

PREP TIME
**15 mins**

COOK TIME
**45 mins**

MAKES
**12 slices**

SERVING SIZE
**1 slice**

7 large eggs, room temperature

2 cups almond flour

1 tsp baking powder

½ tsp sea salt

½ tsp xanthan gum

¼ cup olive oil

3oz (90g) salted butter

**1.** Set the air fryer temp to 360°F (180°C). Spray an 8-inch (20cm) square pan with nonstick cooking spray.

**2.** In a large bowl, combine the eggs, almond flour, baking powder, and salt. Mix well. Add the xanthan gum, olive oil, and butter. Mix well to combine. Place the mixture in the pan.

**3.** Place the pan in the fryer basket and bake until the top is golden and a skewer comes out clean from the middle, about 45 minutes.

**4.** Remove the pan from the fryer basket and allow the bread to cool for 10 minutes. Slice into 12 slices before serving.

 **Tips** Using room temperature eggs is the key to helping this bread taste less like eggs. This significantly reduces the release of sulfur from the cooking eggs. Store the baked bread in an airtight container in the fridge for up to 4 days or in the freezer for up to 2 months.

# Cheese & Garlic Rolls

Bread rolls might have seemed like a food from your past, but just because you're following a low-carb diet doesn't mean you can't have a delicious cheesy roll.

**NUTRITION PER 1 ROLL:**
**153** CALORIES
**12g** TOTAL FAT
**3g** NET CARBS
**7g** PROTEIN
**3g** DIETARY FIBER

PREP TIME
**10 mins**

COOK TIME
**11 mins**

MAKES
**4 rolls**

SERVING SIZE
**1 roll**

½ cup almond flour

1 tbsp psyllium husk powder

1 tsp baking powder

1 tbsp apple cider vinegar

1 large egg white

⅓ cup hot water

1 tsp garlic powder

½ cup grated Cheddar cheese

**1.** Set the air fryer temp to 360°F (180°C).

**2.** In a medium bowl, combine the almond flour, psyllium husk powder, and baking powder. Mix well.

**3.** Add the apple cider vinegar and egg white. Mix until the ingredients start to come together. Add the hot water and continue to mix until the ingredients absorb all the hot water and turn into a dough ball.

**4.** Split the dough into quarters and roll into balls. Place the balls on a baking pan.

**5.** Place the pan in the fryer basket and bake until the balls double in size and have a crispy exterior, about 10 minutes. Remove the pan from the fryer basket.

**6.** In a small bowl, combine the garlic powder and Cheddar cheese. Cover the balls with the mixture. Return the pan to the fryer basket and cook until the cheese has melted, about 1 to 2 minutes more.

**7.** Remove the pan from the fryer basket and allow the rolls to cool for 2 minutes before serving.

**Tips** The water needs to be hot for this recipe to work properly because psyllium husk powder activates with hot water to create perfect rolls. Store the baked rolls in an airtight container in the fridge for up to 7 days or in the freezer for up to 1 month.

# Creamed Spinach

This zesty creamed spinach might not be your traditional take on this recipe, but it's one I've made for years and have adapted for the air fryer.

**NUTRITION PER ¼ CUP:**

**115** CALORIES
**11g** TOTAL FAT
**2g** NET CARBS
**3g** PROTEIN
**2g** DIETARY FIBER

PREP TIME
**5 mins**

COOK TIME
**13 mins**

MAKES
**1 cup**

SERVING SIZE
**¼ cup**

1 tbsp salted butter

2 garlic cloves, minced

¼ tsp sea salt, plus more

¼ tsp ground black pepper, plus more

½ cup heavy whipping cream

1 tbsp apple cider vinegar

1 tsp Dijon mustard

3 cups fresh organic spinach, washed, divided

**1.** Set the air fryer temp to 360°F (180°C).

**2.** Place the butter, garlic, salt, and pepper on a rimmed baking pan. Place the pan in the fryer basket and cook until the garlic is fragrant, about 2 minutes. Remove the pan from the fryer basket.

**3.** Add the whipping cream, apple cider vinegar, and Dijon mustard. Mix well.

**4.** Place 1 cup of spinach on the pan and mix, covering with as much of the cream mixture as possible. Return the pan to the fryer basket and cook until the spinach has begun to wilt, about 3 minutes more. Repeat this step with the remaining spinach until all the spinach has been added. Cook until the spinach has cooked and the cream has reduced slightly, about 5 minutes more.

**5.** Remove the pan from the fryer basket and transfer the creamed spinach to a serving bowl. Top with more salt and pepper (if using) before serving.

**Tips** Spinach often gets sprayed with a lot of chemicals when it's grown commercially, so if you can afford organic spinach, this is definitely a healthy option and often the best use of your money when it comes to buying organic vegetables. Store the cooked spinach in an airtight container in the fridge for up to 4 days.

# Fried Cauliflower Rice

Cauliflower is a versatile staple of the keto kitchen. This recipe shows you how to turn this vegetable into the best-tasting fried rice.

**NUTRITION PER 1 CUP:**

**160** CALORIES
**14g** TOTAL FAT
**4g** NET CARBS
**5g** PROTEIN
**3g** DIETARY FIBER

PREP TIME
**10 mins**

COOK TIME
**10 mins**

MAKES
**4 cups**

SERVING SIZE
**1 cup**

1 tbsp salted butter

2 tbsp olive oil

2 garlic cloves, minced

½ large head of cauliflower, riced (about 5 cups)

2 tbsp tamari (or gluten-free soy sauce)

1 large egg, whisked

1 tbsp sesame seed oil

¼ cup green onions, tops only, sliced

1 lemon

**1.** Set the air fryer temp to 400°F (200°C).

**2.** Place the butter, olive oil, and garlic on a baking pan. Place the pan in the fryer basket and cook until the garlic becomes fragrant, about 3 minutes. Remove the pan from the fryer basket. Add the cauliflower and mix well to evenly coat the cauliflower.

**3.** Return the pan to the fryer basket and cook until the cauliflower softens, about 5 minutes more, stirring every 2 minutes. Remove the pan from the fryer basket.

**4.** Add the soy sauce, egg, sesame seed oil, and green onions. Stir well. Return the pan to the fryer basket and cook until the cauliflower is soft and fragrant, about 2 minutes more.

**5.** Remove the pan from the fryer basket and allow the rice to cool for 2 minutes. Squeeze a little lemon juice over the top before serving.

 **Tips** Diced bacon also goes well with this recipe. Store the fried rice in an airtight container in the fridge for up to 4 days or in the freezer for up to 1 month.

# Cauliflower au Gratin

Instead of potato, this recipe uses cauliflower, which has less carbs but contains plenty of vitamins C, K, and B6—all important for a healthy energy system.

**NUTRITION PER ½ CUP:**

**377** CALORIES
**33g** TOTAL FAT
**6g** NET CARBS
**15g** PROTEIN
**1g** DIETARY FIBER

PREP TIME
**10 mins**

COOK TIME
**23 mins**

MAKES
**2 cups**

SERVING SIZE
**½ cup**

½ head of cauliflower

3 tbsp salted butter, melted

¼ cup heavy whipping cream

¼ cup almond milk

¼ tsp smoked paprika

½ tsp onion powder

¼ tsp ground black pepper

2 cups grated Cheddar cheese

**1.** Set the air fryer temp to 360°F (180°C).

**2.** Cut the cauliflower into 2 slices, each about ¾ inch (2cm) thick. Place the slices on a rimmed baking pan and add enough water to just cover them.

**3.** Place the pan in the fryer basket and cook until tender, about 15 minutes. Remove the pan from the fryer basket, drain the water, and set the slices aside.

**4.** Raise the air fryer temp to 400°F (200°C).

**5.** In a medium bowl, combine the butter, whipping cream, almond milk, paprika, onion powder, and pepper. Pour this into the pan. Return the pan to the fryer basket and cook for 5 minutes more, stirring halfway through. Remove the pan from the fryer basket and set aside.

**6.** Lower the air fryer temp to 360°F (180°C).

**7.** Add the cauliflower to the pan and cover with cheese. Return the pan to the fryer basket and cook until the cheese has melted and turned slightly golden, about 3 minutes.

**8.** Remove the pan from the fryer basket and allow the gratin to cool for 5 minutes before serving.

 **Tips** You can also cook the cauliflower in boiling water on the stovetop until softened. Store the cooked au gratin in an airtight container in the fridge for up to 4 days or in the freezer for up to 1 month.

# Loaded Zucchini

Celebrate zucchini with a delightful mix of Cheddar cheese, bacon, and green onions. This is a great way to add vegetables to your diet without much effort.

**NUTRITION PER 1 ZUCCHINI:**

**280** CALORIES
**20g** TOTAL FAT
**9g** NET CARBS
**17g** PROTEIN
**3g** DIETARY FIBER

PREP TIME
**10 mins**

COOK TIME
**15 mins**

MAKES
**2 zucchini**

SERVING SIZE
**1 zucchini**

2 large zucchini

2 thin slices of bacon

½ cup grated Cheddar cheese

2 tbsp sour cream

2 tbsp chopped green onions

¼ tsp paprika

¼ tsp ground black pepper

**1.** Set the air fryer temp to 360°F (180°C).

**2.** Cut the zucchini in half and remove the seeds using a spoon. Cut the zucchini into 2-inch (5cm) pieces.

**3.** Place the zucchini skin side down in the fryer basket and cook until slightly soft, about 5 minutes. Remove the zucchini from the fryer basket and set aside.

**4.** Place the bacon in the fryer basket and cook until crispy, about 5 minutes. Remove the bacon from the fryer basket and dice into small pieces.

**5.** In a medium bowl, combine the Cheddar cheese, sour cream, green onions, paprika, pepper, and bacon. Place an equal amount of the mixture on each zucchini. Place the zucchini on a baking pan.

**6.** Place the pan in the fryer basket and cook until the cheese has melted, about 5 minutes.

**7.** Remove the pan from the fryer basket and allow the zucchini to cool for 2 minutes before serving.

**Tips** This can be a side dish to a delicious seafood main meal or it can even be a main dish accompanied with a big summer salad. Store the cooked zucchini in an airtight container in the fridge for up to 3 days.

# Ratatouille

Originating from France's southern coast, ratatouille is a stewed vegetable dish made with fresh summer vegetables and plenty of rich olive oil and herbs.

NUTRITION PER
1 CUP:

**117** CALORIES
**8g** TOTAL FAT
**8g** NET CARBS
**3g** PROTEIN
**5g** DIETARY FIBER

PREP TIME
**10 mins**

COOK TIME
**30 mins**

MAKES
**6 cups**

SERVING SIZE
**1 cup**

½ large eggplant (aubergine), roughly chopped

1 zucchini, roughly chopped

½ red bell pepper, seeds removed, chopped

½ red onion, chopped

3 tbsp olive oil

3 garlic cloves, minced

1¼ cups canned crushed tomatoes

2 fresh tomatoes, chopped

1 tsp dried basil

1 tsp dried rosemary

1 tsp sea salt, plus more

½ tsp ground black pepper, plus more

**1.** Set the air fryer temp to 360°F (180°C).

**2.** In a large bowl, combine the eggplant, zucchini, bell pepper, red onion, and olive oil. Mix well to coat. Place the vegetables on a baking pan.

**3.** Place the pan in the air fryer and cook until the eggplant is a little soft and the onion is fragrant, about 10 minutes, mixing halfway through to get even browning. Remove the pan from the fryer basket.

**4.** Add the garlic, canned tomatoes, fresh tomatoes, basil, rosemary, salt, and pepper to the pan. Mix well until combined. Return the pan to the fryer basket and cook until the tomato liquid has reduced, about 15 minutes more, stirring every 5 minutes.

**5.** Remove the pan from the fryer basket and allow the ratatouille to cool for 3 minutes. Spoon the ratatouille into bowls and season with more salt and pepper before serving.

**Tips** Ratatouille pairs well with any kind of roasted meat, especially seared chicken. You can also top it with a little crumbled goat cheese and enjoy it on a slice of keto toast to really indulge. Store the cooked ratatouille in an airtight container in the fridge for up to 4 days or in the freezer for up to 1 month.

# Lemon & Garlic Zucchini Noodles

This simple yet delicious flavor combination of lemon, garlic, and zucchini noodles adds freshness and zest to a side dish perfect for any main meal.

**NUTRITION PER ½ CUP:**

**175** CALORIES
**15g** TOTAL FAT
**5g** NET CARBS
**5g** PROTEIN
**2g** DIETARY FIBER

PREP TIME
**10 mins**

COOK TIME
**4 mins**

MAKES
**2 cups**

SERVING SIZE
**½ cup**

2 tbsp olive oil

2 tbsp salted butter

3 garlic cloves, crushed

3 large zucchini

2 tbsp freshly squeezed lemon juice

4 tbsp grated Parmesan cheese

¼ tsp sea salt

½ tsp ground black pepper

**1.** Set the air fryer temp to 360°F (180°C).

**2.** Spiralize the zucchini. Place the zucchini on a plate lined with paper towels. Use more paper towels to press down to remove all the excess liquid from the zucchini. Try to get them as dry as possible.

**3.** Place the olive oil, butter, and garlic on a baking pan. Place the pan in the fryer basket and cook until the garlic has become fragrant, about 3 minutes.

**4.** Remove the pan from the fryer basket and add the noodles, lemon juice, and Parmesan. Stir until the noodles are well coated.

**5.** Return the pan to the fryer basket and cook until the noodles are tender, about 1 minute more.

**6.** Remove the pan from the fryer basket and season the noodles with salt and pepper before serving.

 **Tips** You can also replace the Parmesan with the same amount of nutritional yeast flakes and substitute the butter with more olive oil. This dish is best eaten fresh.

# Snacks

# Zucchini Rounds

Zucchini rounds are super easy to make because they require no breading, egg wash, or other complications. Top these with any kind of herb seasoning you love.

PREP TIME
**10 mins**

COOK TIME
**20 mins**

MAKES
**¾ cup**

SERVING SIZE
**¾ cup**

1 large zucchini
¼ tsp sea salt, plus more
1 tsp olive oil
¼ tsp ground black pepper

**1.** Set the air fryer temp to 360°F (180°C).

**2.** Use a mandoline or sharp knife to cut the zucchini into ⅛-inch (3mm) rounds. Place the zucchini and salt in a large bowl. Mix to coat and allow to rest for 5 minutes.

Place the zucchini on a plate lined with paper towels. Use more paper towels to press down to remove all the excess liquid from the zucchini. Try to get them as dry as possible.

**3.** In a clean large bowl, combine the zucchini and olive oil. Mix well to coat.

**4.** Working in batches, place half the zucchini in the fryer basket and cook until crispy, about 10 minutes, flipping halfway through.

**5.** Remove the rounds from the fryer basket and allow to cool slightly. Season with salt and pepper before serving.

 **Tips** If you're looking for suggestions, everything bagel seasoning is delicious on these chips. A sugar-free rib rub can also be a winner. The cooked zucchini is best eaten fresh.

# Roasted Nut Butter

Almonds contain healthy fats, fiber, protein, vitamin E, and magnesium. Plus, quite honestly, they seem to taste better when roasted in an air fryer!

**NUTRITION PER 1 TABLESPOON:**

**90** CALORIES
**8g** TOTAL FAT
**1g** NET CARBS
**3g** PROTEIN
**2g** DIETARY FIBER

| PREP TIME | COOK TIME | MAKES | SERVING SIZE |
|---|---|---|---|
| **20 mins** | **10 mins** | **1¼ cups** | **1 tablespoon** |

2 cups raw almonds (10oz [285g])

3 tbsp coconut oil

½ tsp sea salt

**1.** Set the air fryer temp to 360°F (180°C).

**2.** Place the almonds on a baking pan. Place the pan in the fryer basket and roast until the almonds have turned golden and feel slightly oily to the touch, about 10 minutes.

**3.** Remove the pan from the fryer basket and allow the almonds to cool for 20 minutes.

**4.** Place the almonds in a food processor and blend on high until a paste begins to form. Add the coconut oil and salt. Continue to blend until smooth.

**5.** Transfer the butter to a jar. Refrigerate for a thicker butter.

**Tips** Because the coconut oil can find its way to the top of the jar during storage, be sure to give the oil on top of the butter a quick mix through so you have a consistent flavor all the way through the jar. Store the jar in a cool, dry place for up to 2 weeks.

# Avocado Fries

These fries will impress keto enthusiasts who love crunchy and creamy textures in one bite. Using pork rinds will help you give this dish that crispy quality.

**NUTRITION PER ¼ AVOCADO:**

**155** CALORIES
**13g** TOTAL FAT
**1g** NET CARBS
**6g** PROTEIN
**2g** DIETARY FIBER

PREP TIME
**10 mins**

COOK TIME
**20 mins**

MAKES
**1 avocado**

SERVING SIZE
**¼ avocado**

1 tbsp olive oil mayonnaise

1 tsp yellow mustard

1 large egg

½ cup pork panko breadcrumbs (or ground pork crackle)

1 ripe but firm avocado, sliced

¼ lemon, sliced

**1.** Set the air fryer temp to 400°F (200°C). Spray the fryer basket with nonstick cooking spray.

**2.** In a small bowl, combine the mayonnaise and mustard. Place the sauce in a dipping bowl and set aside.

**3.** In a separate small bowl, whisk the egg. Place the pork panko breadcrumbs in another small bowl. Dip the avocado slices in the egg and then in the breadcrumbs. Ensure an even coating.

**4.** Working in batches, place half the avocado in the fryer basket and cook until the breadcrumbs are golden brown, about 10 minutes, flipping halfway through.

**5.** Remove the fries from the fryer basket. Serve immediately with the dipping sauce and lemon slices.

 **Tip** These avocado fries are best eaten fresh—they'll go soggy if stored in the fridge.

# Candied Bacon

These bacon slices are covered with a candied cinnamon coating, infusing the pork with smokiness and a warm-spiced sweetness.

**NUTRITION PER 2 SLICES:**

**135** CALORIES
**11g** TOTAL FAT
**1g** NET CARBS
**9g** PROTEIN
**1g** DIETARY FIBER

PREP TIME
**5 mins**

COOK TIME
**5 mins**

MAKES
**4 slices**

SERVING SIZE
**2 slices**

1 tsp ghee

2 tbsp golden erythritol sweetener

½ tsp ground cinnamon

4 slices of bacon (2oz [60g])

**1.** Set the air fryer temp to 360°F (180°C). Coat the fryer basket with the ghee.

**2.** In a small bowl, combine the erythritol and cinnamon. Mix well. Cover both sides of the bacon with the cinnamon mixture.

**3.** Place the bacon in the fryer basket and cook until crispy, about 5 minutes.

**4.** Remove the bacon from the fryer basket and allow to cool for 1 minute before serving.

**Tips** Pair this bacon with pancakes. If you're unable to find a brown sugar substitute like golden erythritol, regular erythritol will also work fine—it just won't have the malted taste that brown sugar gives. Store the cooked bacon in an airtight container in the fridge for up to 4 days.

# Bacon-Wrapped Avocado

Let's face it: Wrapping every food in bacon can get old. But trust me on this—avocado is the only ingredient you'll want to wrap in bacon after trying this dish!

**NUTRITION PER 2 SLICES:**

**195** CALORIES
**17g** TOTAL FAT
**1g** NET CARBS
**9g** PROTEIN
**2g** DIETARY FIBER

| PREP TIME | COOK TIME | MAKES | SERVING SIZE |
|-----------|-----------|-------|--------------|
| **10 mins** | **10 mins** | **4 slices** | **2 slices** |

1 tsp coconut oil
½ ripe but firm avocado
2 slices of bacon (2oz [60g])
sea salt
ground black pepper

**1.** Set the air fryer temp to 400°F (200°C). Coat the fryer basket with the coconut oil.

**2.** Cut the avocado into 4 slices. Wrap each piece in half a slice of bacon or enough to fully cover.

**3.** Working in batches, place 2 avocado slices in the fryer basket and cook until the bacon becomes crispy, about 5 minutes, flipping halfway through.

**4.** Remove the slices from the fryer basket and allow to cool for 1 minute. Season with salt and pepper before serving.

 **Tip** These avocado slices are best eaten fresh—they'll go soggy if stored in the fridge.

# Breaded Calamari
## with Tangy Aioli

Breaded calamari is usually served with French fries (called *chips* where I'm from in Australia), but you could pair this with a fresh zesty salad or white wine.

**NUTRITION PER 5 CALAMARI RINGS + 2 TABLESPOONS AIOLI:**

**517** CALORIES
**40g** TOTAL FAT
**4g** NET CARBS
**35g** PROTEIN
**3g** DIETARY FIBER

PREP TIME
**10 mins**

COOK TIME
**16 mins**

MAKES
**10 calamari rings**

SERVING SIZE
**5 calamari rings + 2 tablespoons of aioli**

½ cup almond flour

2 tbsp unflavored whey protein powder

½ tsp dried parsley

½ tsp dried basil

½ tsp sea salt

¼ tsp ground black pepper

1 large egg

2 squid tubes (9oz [255g])

½ lemon, sliced

**for the aioli**

4 tbsp mayonnaise

½ tsp Dijon mustard

1 garlic clove, minced

**1.** Set the air fryer temp to 400°F (200°C). Spray the fryer basket with nonstick cooking spray.

**2.** In a small bowl, make the aioli by combining the mayonnaise, mustard, and garlic. Set aside.

**3.** In a medium bowl, combine the almond flour, protein powder, parsley, basil, salt, and pepper. In a small bowl, whisk the egg.

**4.** Cut the squid tubes horizontally into ½-inch (1.25cm) calamari rings. Dip each slice in the egg and then in the flour mixture.

**5.** Working in batches, place half the rings in the fryer basket and ensure ample room for air around each piece. Cook until golden and crispy, about 8 minutes.

**6.** Remove the calamari from the fryer basket. Serve immediately with the aioli and lemon slices.

**Tips** Cooked calamari is best eaten fresh because the breading doesn't stay crispy when it cools. Make small batches of uncooked breaded squid if you want to freeze this recipe for later.

# Buffalo Cauliflower Bites

Cauliflower is great for increasing antioxidant intake, reducing inflammation, and improving your gut health. Plus, these bites have a spicy taste you'll enjoy.

**NUTRITION PER 1 CUP:**

**70** CALORIES
**6g** TOTAL FAT
**3g** NET CARBS
**2g** PROTEIN
**2g** DIETARY FIBER

PREP TIME
**5 mins**

COOK TIME
**10 mins**

MAKES
**4 cups**

SERVING SIZE
**1 cup**

¼ cup hot sauce (Frank's RedHot or similar)

2 tbsp salted butter, melted

1 tsp sea salt

1 tsp ground black pepper

½ large head of cauliflower, cut into florets

**1.** Set the air fryer temp to 400°F (200°C).

**2.** In a small bowl, combine all the ingredients except the cauliflower.

**3.** In a large bowl, place the cauliflower. Pour the hot sauce mixture over the cauliflower and mix with clean hands until well coated.

**4.** Place the cauliflower in the fryer basket and cook for 10 minutes or until your desired tenderness has been reached.

**5.** Transfer the bites to a platter and serve immediately.

 **Tips** If you'd like to make your own hot sauce, you can use a combination of vinegar, hot peppers, and garlic. Store the cooked cauliflower in an airtight container in the fridge for up to 7 days or in the freezer for up to 2 months.

# Crispy Cauliflower Bites

You'll use ground herbs to crisp up these bites without adding carbs. The Middle Eastern–inspired flavor combination will keep you satisfied for hours.

**NUTRITION PER 1 CUP:**

**230** CALORIES
**15g** TOTAL FAT
**5g** NET CARBS
**15g** PROTEIN
**5g** DIETARY FIBER

| PREP TIME | COOK TIME | MAKES | SERVING SIZE |
|---|---|---|---|
| **10 mins** | **10 mins** | **2 cups** | **1 cup** |

½ **large head of cauliflower (14oz [400g]), cut into florets**

2 **tbsp olive oil**

½ **tsp ground cumin**

½ **tsp ground cinnamon**

½ **tsp dried cilantro (coriander)**

½ **tsp sea salt**

½ **tsp ground black pepper**

**1.** Set the air fryer temp to 400°F (200°C).

**2.** In a large bowl, combine the florets and olive oil. Mix well to coat.

**3.** In a small bowl, combine the ground cumin, ground cinnamon, cilantro, salt, and pepper. Mix until uniform in color. Add to the cauliflower and stir well to ensure the cauliflower has a light coating.

**4.** Place the cauliflower in the fryer basket and cook for 10 minutes or until the outsides have reached your desired level of crispiness.

**5.** Transfer the cauliflower bites to a platter and serve immediately.

 **Tip** Store the cooked cauliflower bites in an airtight container in the fridge for up to 7 days or in the freezer for up to 2 months.

# Coconut Shrimp

This is a fantastic snack to air-fry because you can get the coconut coating nice and crispy. Get creative with sauces by using your favorite flavor pairings.

**NUTRITION PER 4oz (120g):**

**383** CALORIES
**27g** TOTAL FAT
**5g** NET CARBS
**30g** PROTEIN
**5g** DIETARY FIBER

PREP TIME
**10 mins**

COOK TIME
**36 mins**

MAKES
**8oz (255g)**

SERVING SIZE
**4oz (120g)**

1 cup unsweetened desiccated coconut

1 tsp dried basil

1 tsp garlic powder

¼ tsp sea salt

¼ tsp ground black pepper

1 large egg

7oz (200g) shrimp (about 15 to 20), peeled and deveined

**1.** Set the air fryer temp to 360°F (180°C). Spray the fryer basket with nonstick cooking spray.

**2.** In a medium bowl, combine the coconut, basil, garlic powder, salt, and pepper. In a small bowl, whisk the egg.

**3.** Dip the shrimp in the egg and then in the coconut mixture. Ensure an even coating.

**4.** Working in batches, place half the shrimp in the fryer basket and cook until crispy, about 18 minutes, flipping halfway through.

**5.** Remove the shrimp from the fryer basket and allow to cool for 2 minutes before serving.

**Tips** Coconut shrimp pairs well with bacon, chives, and jalapeños, but you can also create a fancy dipping sauce of choice or add the shrimp to your favorite steak dinner as a topper. Store the cooked shrimp in an airtight container in the fridge for up to 2 days, although for maximum crispness, these are best eaten fresh.

# Kale Chips

Let's be honest: Kale needs help to make it delicious. I've done all the hard work for you and created the best-tasting kale chips ever made with an air fryer.

**NUTRITION PER 1 CUP:**

**75** CALORIES
**7g** TOTAL FAT
**1g** NET CARBS
**1g** PROTEIN
**1g** DIETARY FIBER

PREP TIME
**10 mins**

COOK TIME
**3 mins**

MAKES
**2 cups**

SERVING SIZE
**1 cup**

6 large stalks of kale (2 cups chopped)

1 tbsp olive oil

½ garlic clove, finely minced

¼ lemon

¼ tsp sea salt

**1.** Set the air fryer temp to 360°F (180°C).

**2.** Cut the kale horizontally into 2½-inch (6.25cm) pieces and remove the stalks. In a large bowl, combine the kale, olive oil, and garlic. Mix well until the leaves are coated.

**3.** Place the kale in the fryer basket and cook until the leaves are crispy and cooked through, about 3 minutes.

**4.** Transfer the kale to a serving bowl. Squeeze a little lemon juice over the top and season with the salt before serving.

 **Tips** If you have access to smoked salt, the bittersweet zest from the kale pairs perfectly with a smoky salt flavor. Store the cooked kale in an airtight container in the fridge for up to 4 days.

# Salami Chips

Craving crisp snacks on keto? These salami chips are a fantastic addition to a cheese board or to a selection of dips—and they're ready in 3 minutes!

**NUTRITION PER 5 CHIPS:**

**225** CALORIES
**19g** TOTAL FAT
**1g** NET CARBS
**13g** PROTEIN
**0g** DIETARY FIBER

PREP TIME
**2 mins**

COOK TIME
**3 mins**

MAKES
**5 chips**

SERVING SIZE
**5 chips**

5 thin slices of salami (2oz [60g])

**1.** Set the air fryer temp to 400°F (200°C).

**2.** Place the salami in the fryer basket and ensure even spacing between the slices. Cook until crispy, about 3 minutes.

**3.** Transfer the salami to a paper towel to cool slightly before serving.

 **Tips** Thin-sliced deli salami that's large in diameter works best for this recipe because thick salami will inhibit crispness. Store the cooked salami in an airtight container in the fridge for up to 4 days or in the freezer for up to 1 month.

# Cheese Crackers

These crackers are crispy, ideally seasoned, and, yes, cheesy. They're a perfect addition to your snack plate or enjoy them with your favorite spreads and sauces.

**NUTRITION PER 8 CRACKERS:**

**200** CALORIES
**16g** TOTAL FAT
**3g** NET CARBS
**10g** PROTEIN
**2g** DIETARY FIBER

PREP TIME
**10 mins**

COOK TIME
**20 mins**

MAKES
**16 crackers**

SERVING SIZE
**8 crackers**

⅓ cup almond flour

¼ tsp sea salt

¼ tsp ground black pepper

¼ tsp dried basil

¼ tsp dried parsley

½ large egg, whisked

1 tbsp finely grated Parmesan cheese

2 tbsp grated Cheddar cheese

**1.** Set the air fryer temp to 360°F (180°C). Spray the fryer basket with nonstick cooking spray.

**2.** In a medium bowl, combine the almond flour, salt, pepper, basil, and parsley. Mix until uniform in color.

**3.** Add the egg to the flour mixture and mix well. Add the Parmesan and press the cheese into the mixture, folding as best as you can.

**4.** Place the mixture between two sheets of parchment paper and roll the dough out to ¼ inch (0.5cm) thick. Cut the dough into fourths and then cut each fourth into fourths, for 16 total squares.

**5.** Working in batches, place 8 squares in the fryer basket, leaving a little room around each square so they don't stick together. Cook until golden brown and crispy, about 10 minutes.

**6.** Remove the crackers from the fryer basket and allow to cool for 2 minutes before serving.

 **Tips** Double the recipe to use the rest of the egg. Try to only make enough to have in one sitting because the crispy texture doesn't keep well once the crackers have been left sitting too long.

# Mozzarella Sticks

Mozzarella lends itself well to air frying because the stringy, stretchy properties hold their shape while cooking but have a delightful softness with each bite.

**NUTRITION PER 6 STICKS:**

**367** CALORIES
**27g** TOTAL FAT
**4g** NET CARBS
**28g** PROTEIN
**2g** DIETARY FIBER

PREP TIME
**30 mins**

COOK TIME
**10 mins**

MAKES
**24 sticks**

SERVING SIZE
**6 sticks**

10oz (285g) mozzarella cheese sticks (about 12 sticks), sliced in half

½ cup almond flour

2 tbsp unflavored whey protein powder

1 tsp dried parsley

½ tsp dried basil

¼ tsp sea salt

¼ tsp ground black pepper

1 large egg

**1.** Set the air fryer temp to 360°F (180°C). Spray the fryer basket with nonstick cooking spray.

**2.** Place the mozzarella in a freezer bag and freeze for 30 minutes.

**3.** In a medium bowl, combine the almond flour, protein powder, parsley, basil, salt, and pepper. In a small bowl, whisk the egg.

**4.** Dip each cheese stick in the egg and then in the flour mixture. Place the sticks on a plate and freeze again for 10 minutes.

**5.** Coat each stick again in the flour mixture, double-coating them, and return the sticks to the freezer for 10 minutes more to set.

**6.** Working in batches, place 12 sticks in the fryer basket and cook until crispy and golden brown on the outside, about 5 minutes, flipping halfway through.

**7.** Remove the sticks from the fryer basket and serve immediately.

 **Tips** If you don't have whey protein powder, you can substitute finely grated Parmesan, but the sticks won't get quite as crispy. These are best eaten fresh because they'll go soggy in the fridge. Store uncooked mozzarella sticks in the freezer for up to 2 months.

# Cheese Scones

Scones are typically a sweet bread, but this recipe uses savory Cheddar cheese and zesty herbs to create an appetizing snack that's nutritious and low in carbs.

**NUTRITION PER 1 SCONE:**

**118** CALORIES
**10g** TOTAL FAT
**2g** NET CARBS
**3g** PROTEIN
**2g** DIETARY FIBER

PREP TIME
**10 mins**

COOK TIME
**8 mins**

MAKES
**8 scones**

SERVING SIZE
**1 scone**

1 cup almond flour

2 tbsp coconut flour

¼ tsp sea salt

¼ tsp garlic powder

¼ tsp xanthan gum

½ tsp dried basil

2 tbsp plus 1½ tsp salted butter, melted

3 tbsp grated Cheddar cheese

**1.** Set the air fryer temp to 320°F (160°C). Spray the fryer basket with nonstick cooking spray.

**2.** In a medium bowl, combine all the ingredients until well mixed and the mixture forms a dough. Roll the dough into 8 balls.

**3.** Place the balls in the fryer basket and bake until slightly golden brown on the outside, about 8 minutes.

**4.** Remove the balls from the fryer basket and allow to cool for 5 minutes. Cut the balls in half to form the scones before serving with your favorite toppings.

 **Tip** Store the baked scones in an airtight container in the fridge for up to 5 days or in the freezer for up to 1 month.

# Stuffed Jalapeño Poppers

These jalapeño poppers are a fantastic way to enjoy the perfect bite. Heat paired with the creamy cheese filling will make these an absolute crowd-pleaser.

**NUTRITION PER 10 POPPERS:**

**390** CALORIES
**34g** TOTAL FAT
**7g** NET CARBS
**10g** PROTEIN
**3g** DIETARY FIBER

PREP TIME
**10 mins**

COOK TIME
**10 mins**

MAKES
**20 poppers**

SERVING SIZE
**10 poppers**

6oz (170g) full-fat cream cheese, room temperature

¼ cup grated Parmesan cheese

1 tbsp dried onion flakes

½ tsp paprika

¼ tsp sea salt

½ tsp ground black pepper

10 fresh jalapeños (or mini bell peppers), seeds removed, cut in half

1 tbsp grated mozzarella cheese

**1.** Set the air fryer temp to 360°F (180°C). Spray the fryer basket with nonstick cooking spray.

**2.** In a medium bowl, combine the cream cheese, Parmesan, onion flakes, paprika, salt, and pepper. Mix well. Spoon the mixture into the jalapeños and top each half with an equal amount of mozzarella.

**3.** Working in batches, place 10 jalapeños in the fryer basket and cook until the cheese on top is golden and the jalapeños have slightly softened, about 5 minutes.

**4.** Remove the poppers from the fryer basket and serve immediately.

 **Tips** If you love the flavor and heat of a chili pepper, I recommend adding half the seeds from the jalapeños to the cheese mixture. This gives the recipe a real kick. Store the cooked poppers in an airtight container in the fridge for up to 4 days, although they're best eaten fresh.

# Feta Psiti

This traditional Greek recipe gets an air fryer spin. Serve this simple yet elegant baked feta dish with crackers, sliced meats, and other cheeses.

**NUTRITION PER ¼ BLOCK OF FETA:**

**123** CALORIES
**11g** TOTAL FAT
**2g** NET CARBS
**5g** PROTEIN
**0g** DIETARY FIBER

PREP TIME
**5 mins**

COOK TIME
**10 mins**

MAKES
**1 block of feta**

SERVING SIZE
**¼ block of feta**

¼ tsp dried parsley

¼ tsp dried basil

¼ tsp dried oregano

¼ tsp chili powder

1 tsp erythritol sweetener (golden recommended)

1 tbsp olive oil

5oz (140g) block of feta cheese

**1.** Set the air fryer temp to 360°F (180°C). Spray a baking pan with nonstick cooking spray.

**2.** In a small bowl, combine the parsley, basil, oregano, chili powder, erythritol, and olive oil. Place the feta in the pan and add the herb mixture. Mix well to coat.

**3.** Place the pan in the fryer basket and bake until the feta becomes soft, about 10 minutes.

**4.** Remove the pan from the fryer basket and allow the feta to cool for 1 minute before serving.

**Tips** You can substitute the erythritol with any keto-friendly sweetener. This would equate to around 4 to 5 drops of stevia, but if you're not too worried about the carb content, 1 teaspoon of honey would add 5 grams of total carbs to the recipe. Store the baked feta in an airtight container in the fridge for up to 4 days or in the freezer for up to 1 month.

# Cauliflower Tots

This is a delectable recipe to make in the air fryer and much healthier for you because you won't have to cook these tots in hydrogenated vegetable oils.

**NUTRITION PER 12 TOTS:**

**210** CALORIES
**18g** TOTAL FAT
**4g** NET CARBS
**6g** PROTEIN
**3g** DIETARY FIBER

PREP TIME
**10 mins**

COOK TIME
**30 mins**

MAKES
**24 tots**

SERVING SIZE
**12 tots**

2 tbsp ghee, divided

1 cup cauliflower rice

½ cup water

¼ cup grated mozzarella cheese

1 tbsp grated Parmesan cheese

2 tbsp coconut flour

¼ tsp sea salt

½ tsp ground black pepper

**1.** Set the air fryer temp to 360°F (180°C). Coat the fryer basket with the ghee.

**2.** In a large bowl, combine the cauliflower rice, water, mozzarella, Parmesan, coconut flour, salt, and pepper. Mix well. Set aside for 5 minutes to allow the coconut flour to absorb the water. (You can also mix these ingredients in a food processor.) Form the mixture into 24 tots, about 1 tablespoon each.

**3.** Working in batches, place 12 tots in the fryer basket and ensure ample room for air around each one. Use a pastry brush or sprigs of herbs to coat the tops with a little ghee. Cook until crispy on the outside and golden, about 15 minutes, flipping every 5 minutes and coating with the remaining ghee.

**4.** Remove the tots from the fryer basket and place on paper towels. Allow the tots to cool for 3 minutes before serving.

 **Tips** Australians love coating these snacks with "chicken salt," which is a mixture of 1 part chicken stock cube and 1 part sea salt that forms a seasoned salt that goes perfectly with this snack. The cooked tots are best eaten fresh, but you can also store them in an airtight container lined with paper towels in the fridge for up to 5 days.

# Pizza Bites

This simple take on an appetizer tops a crispy salami cracker with your typical pizza flavorings to bring you a keto snack that's super easy to make and delicious!

**NUTRITION PER 4 PIZZA BITES:**

**170** CALORIES
**13g** TOTAL FAT
**3g** NET CARBS
**11g** PROTEIN
**1g** DIETARY FIBER

PREP TIME
**10 mins**

COOK TIME
**11 mins**

MAKES
**8 bites**

SERVING SIZE
**4 bites**

8 large slices of salami

2 tbsp tomato purée

½ tsp dried oregano

½ tsp dried basil

4 tbsp grated mozzarella cheese

2 tbsp grated Parmesan cheese

**1.** Set the air fryer temp to 400°F (200°C).

**2.** Place the salami on a baking pan. Place the pan in the fryer basket and cook until slightly brown, about 5 minutes.

**3.** Remove the pan from the fryer basket and allow the salami to cool for 2 minutes.

**4.** In a small bowl, combine the tomato purée, oregano, and basil. Place an equal amount of this tomato mixture on each slice of salami and top each slice with an equal amount of the mozzarella and Parmesan cheeses.

**5.** Working in batches, place 4 pizza bites in the fryer basket and bake until the cheese has melted, about 3 minutes.

**6.** Remove the bites from the fryer basket and serve immediately.

**Tips** Get creative with added toppings for these pizza bites: shredded chicken and some homemade pesto or a few sliced mushrooms and a few slices of onion. The baked pizza bites are best eaten fresh.

# Pâté

Pâté is considered a superfood among carnivores because it contains plenty of K2, folate, and vitamin C, which can often be lacking in a strict carnivore diet.

**NUTRITION PER 2 TABLESPOONS:**

**120** CALORIES
**10g** TOTAL FAT
**1g** NET CARBS
**7g** PROTEIN
**0g** DIETARY FIBER

PREP TIME
**10 mins**

COOK TIME
**15 mins**

MAKES
**2 cups**

SERVING SIZE
**2 tablespoons**

4oz (120g) salted butter (1 stick), divided

2oz (60g) bacon, diced

½ onion, diced

1 garlic clove, crushed

1 tbsp chopped fresh rosemary

¼ cup white wine

½lb (250g) organic chicken liver

**1.** Set the air fryer temp to 350°F (175°C).

**2.** Dice and refrigerate 3 ounces (90g) of butter (about ¾ of a stick).

**3.** In a baking dish, combine the bacon, onion, garlic, rosemary, white wine, and the remaining 1 ounce (30g) of butter (about ¼ of a stick).

**4.** Place the dish in the fryer basket and cook until the onion becomes translucent and the bacon is crispy, about 7 minutes. Remove the dish from the fryer basket and set aside.

**5.** Raise the air fryer temp to 400°C (200°C).

**6.** Place the chicken liver in the fryer basket and cook until seared on the outside, about 7 minutes.

**7.** Remove the liver from the fryer basket. Allow the bacon mixture and liver to come to room temperature.

**8.** In a high-speed blender, combine the liver and the bacon mixture. Blend until well combined and uniform in color. Add the chilled butter and blend until smooth and uniform in color.

**9.** Transfer the pâté to a serving bowl and serve immediately.

 **Tips** Ensure you buy a good-quality organic liver because this organ processes all the toxins. Substitute white wine with half the amount of white vinegar for a similar taste. Serve these with Cheese Crackers (page 122), Almond Flour Bread (page 96), or your favorite keto-friendly bread. Store the pâté in an airtight container in the fridge for up to 4 days or in the freezer for up to 1 month.

# Breaded Mushrooms

This recipe is one of my absolute favorites from this book, so get ready to be pleasantly surprised with this crispy garlic and mushroom combo.

**NUTRITION PER 3 WHOLE MUSHROOMS:**

**115** CALORIES
**7g** TOTAL FAT
**3g** NET CARBS
**12g** PROTEIN
**2g** DIETARY FIBER

PREP TIME
**10 mins**

COOK TIME
**20 mins**

MAKES
**48 mushroom quarters**

SERVING SIZE
**12 mushroom quarters**

¼ cup almond flour

¼ cup unflavored whey protein powder

1 tsp garlic powder

½ tsp dried parsley

½ tsp dried basil

¼ tsp sea salt

¼ tsp ground black pepper

1 large egg, whisked

1 tsp olive oil

12 large button mushrooms, quartered

**1.** Set the air fryer temp to 400°F (200°C). Spray the fryer basket with nonstick cooking spray.

**2.** In a large freezer bag, combine the almond flour, protein powder, garlic powder, parsley, basil, salt, and pepper. Mix well. In a small bowl, whisk the egg and olive oil.

**3.** Cut the mushrooms into quarters, keeping the stems on. Dip the mushrooms in the egg and then place in the bag with the flour mixture. Shake the bag until the mushrooms are well coated.

**4.** Working in batches, place 24 quarters in the fryer basket and cook until crispy and golden on the outside, about 10 minutes.

**5.** Remove the mushrooms from the fryer basket and allow to cool for 1 minute before serving.

 **Tips** This recipe is best eaten fresh because the breading doesn't stay crispy when it cools. Make small batches of breaded mushrooms if you want to freeze this recipe for later.

# Desserts

# Brownies

These chocolate brownies are dense and rich in flavor, using a secret ingredient to enhance the taste and depth of the chocolate.

NUTRITION PER
1 BROWNIE:

**130** CALORIES
**12g** TOTAL FAT
**4g** NET CARBS
**3g** PROTEIN
**2g** DIETARY FIBER

PREP TIME
**10 mins**

COOK TIME
**25 mins**

MAKES
**15 brownies**

SERVING SIZE
**1 brownie**

½ cup unsweetened baking chocolate (4oz [120g])

½ cup unsalted butter (1 stick)

⅔ cup almond flour

¼ cup Dutch cocoa powder

1 tsp baking powder

½ tsp gelatin powder

1 tsp instant espresso powder

¼ tsp sea salt

3 large eggs

1 cup erythritol sweetener

1 tsp pure vanilla extract

¼ tsp salt flakes

**1.** Set the air fryer temp to 360°F (180°C). Line a baking pan with parchment paper.

**2.** Chop the chocolate into small chunks and place in a heatproof bowl. Microwave the butter until hot and melted all the way through, about 1 minute. Pour the butter over the chocolate. Leave the mixture for 3 minutes to melt the chocolate and then mix.

**3.** In a medium bowl, sift and mix the almond flour, cocoa powder, baking powder, gelatin powder, espresso powder, and salt. Mix until uniform in color.

**4.** In a separate medium bowl, whisk together the eggs, erythritol, and vanilla extract. Slowly add the flour mixture and mix well. Add the chocolate and butter mixture. Mix again until well combined. Place the mixture in the pan.

**5.** Place the pan in the fryer basket and bake for 15 minutes.

**6.** Remove the pan from the fryer basket and evenly distribute the salt flakes over the top. Return the pan to the fryer basket and bake until cooked all the way through, about 5 to 10 minutes. Check for doneness by inserting a skewer into the middle. If the skewer comes out clean, the brownie is done.

**7.** Remove the pan from the fryer basket and allow the brownie to cool for 10 minutes. Slice into 15 slices before serving.

**Tips** These are best served with some cream or a few raspberries. Store the baked brownies in an airtight container in the fridge for up to 7 days or in the freezer for up to 2 months.

# Cheesecake Brownies

This cheesecake uses a chocolate brownie for a base. The chocolate pairs perfectly with the delicate baked cheesecake topping but does require a little work.

**NUTRITION PER ½ BROWNIE:**

**305** CALORIES
**30g** TOTAL FAT
**5g** NET CARBS
**7g** PROTEIN
**4g** DIETARY FIBER

PREP TIME
**10 mins**

COOK TIME
**20 mins**

MAKES
**3 brownies**

SERVING SIZE
**½ brownie**

¼ cup almond flour

3 tbsp unsweetened cocoa powder

½ tsp baking powder

½ tsp gelatin powder

½ tsp instant espresso powder

¼ tsp sea salt

½ block of unsweetened baking chocolate (2oz [60g]), chopped

¼ cup unsalted butter (½ stick), melted

¼ cup erythritol sweetener

**for the topping**

8½oz (240g) cream cheese, room temperature

¼ cup sour cream, room temperature

1 large egg, room temperature

1 tsp pure vanilla extract

¼ cup erythritol sweetener

**1.** Set the air fryer temp to 320°F (160°C). Line an 8-inch (20cm) springform pan with parchment paper.

**2.** In a large bowl, make the topping by combining the cream cheese, sour cream, and egg. Mix using a hand mixer. Add the vanilla extract and erythritol. Mix well. Set aside.

**3.** In a medium bowl, combine the almond flour, cocoa powder, baking powder, gelatin powder, espresso powder, and salt. Mix well.

**4.** Place the chocolate in a medium bowl. Microwave the butter until hot and melted all the way through, about 1 minute. Pour the butter over the chocolate. Leave the mixture for 3 minutes to melt the chocolate. Add the erythritol and mix well.

**5.** Add the dry cocoa mixture to the butter mixture and combine. Reserve 2 tablespoons of this mixture and press the remaining mixture into the bottom of the springform pan.

**6.** Spoon the topping over the brownie mixture. Sprinkle the reserved 2 tablespoons of brownie mixture over the topping. Use a skewer to slightly mix.

**7.** Place the pan in the fryer basket and bake until the topping has fully set, about 20 minutes.

**8.** Remove the pan from the fryer basket and allow the cheesecake to cool to room temperature (or refrigerate overnight) before serving.

💬 **Tips** For the best consistency, ensure your ingredients are all at room temperature before you begin. Otherwise, the cream cheese will clump with the other ingredients and split inside the air fryer. Store the baked cheesecake in an airtight container in the fridge for up to 7 days or in the freezer for up 2 months.

# Giant Chocolate Chip Cookie

Chocolate chip cookies are one of the most popular recipes ever, so why not use the power of an air fryer to make one giant cookie for everyone to share!

**NUTRITION PER ⅛ COOKIE:**

**181** CALORIES
**17g** TOTAL FAT
**3g** NET CARBS
**4g** PROTEIN
**3g** DIETARY FIBER

PREP TIME
**10 mins**

COOK TIME
**15 mins**

MAKES
**1 cookie**

SERVING SIZE
**⅛ cookie**

⅓ cup unsalted butter, melted

¼ cup erythritol sweetener

1 tsp pure vanilla extract

1 large egg

1 cup almond flour

½ tsp baking powder

¼ tsp sea salt

¼ tsp xanthan gum

½ cup sugar-free chocolate chips

**1.** Set the air fryer temp to 360°F (180°C). Line a baking pan with parchment paper.

**2.** In a medium bowl, use a hand mixer to combine the butter, erythritol, and vanilla extract until light and creamy. Add the egg and mix well.

**3.** In a separate medium bowl, combine the almond flour, baking powder, salt, and xanthan gum. Add the butter mixture to the flour mixture. Mix until just combined. Fold in the chocolate chips. Place the dough in the pan and spread it out until even.

**4.** Place the pan in the fryer basket and cook until slightly golden on top, about 15 minutes.

**5.** Remove the pan from the fryer basket and allow the cookie to cool to room temperature. Slice into 8 slices before serving.

**Tips** Feel free to keep a few chocolate chips out of the mixture and place them on top during the cooking process. If you don't have xanthan gum, feel free to leave it out. Store the baked cookie in an airtight container in the fridge for up to 7 days or in the freezer for up to 2 months.

# Snickerdoodle Cookies

Snickerdoodle cookies are typically flavored with cinnamon and maple syrup. This keto alternative is delicious and chewy—and will melt in your mouth.

**NUTRITION PER 1 COOKIE:**

**185** CALORIES
**18g** TOTAL FAT
**2g** NET CARBS
**5g** PROTEIN
**3g** DIETARY FIBER

PREP TIME
**10 mins**

COOK TIME
**6 mins**

MAKES
**7 cookies**

SERVING SIZE
**1 cookie**

1⅓ cup almond flour (5oz [140g])

¼ tsp xanthan gum

¼ tsp baking powder

¼ tsp sea salt

2 tsp ground cinnamon, divided

¼ cup unsalted butter (½ stick), melted

4 tbsp erythritol sweetener, divided

1 large egg, whisked

1 tsp pure vanilla extract

1 fl oz (30ml) sugar-free maple syrup

**1.** Set the air fryer temp to 400°F (200°C). Line a baking pan with parchment paper.

**2.** In a medium bowl, combine the almond flour, xanthan gum, baking powder, salt, and 1 teaspoon of cinnamon. Set aside.

**3.** In a separate medium bowl, use a hand mixer to combine the butter and 2 tablespoons of erythritol until creamy. Add the egg, vanilla extract, and maple syrup. Mix well.

**4.** Fold the wet ingredients into the dry ingredients. Use your hands to form the mixture into 7 balls. Place the balls in the pan and press them down with the back of a fork.

**5.** Place the pan in the fryer basket and bake until slightly golden around the edges, about 5 to 6 minutes.

**6.** In a small bowl, combine the remaining 1 teaspoon of cinnamon and the remaining 2 tablespoons of erythritol.

**7.** Remove the pan from the fryer basket and allow the cookies to come to room temperature. Evenly sprinkle the cinnamon mixture over the cookies before serving.

 **Tips** If you're unable to find sugar-free syrup, any kind of vanilla-flavored sugar-free syrup will work. If you don't have xanthan gum, replace it with ½ teaspoon of gelatin powder. Store the baked cookies in an airtight container in the fridge for up to 7 days.

# Nut Butter Cookies

This recipe is enhanced by the goodness of nut butter. These cookies are easy to make, taste deliciously creamy, and work perfectly as an after-dinner snack.

**NUTRITION PER 1 COOKIE:**

**141** CALORIES
**13g** TOTAL FAT
**3g** NET CARBS
**5g** PROTEIN
**2g** DIETARY FIBER

PREP TIME
**10 mins**

COOK TIME
**6 mins**

MAKES
**6 cookies**

SERVING SIZE
**1 cookie**

1 large egg

7 tbsp salted nut butter of choice

2 tbsp plus 1½ tsp powdered erythritol

2 tbsp plus 1½ tsp salted butter

½ tsp pure vanilla extract

**1.** Set the air fryer temp to 350°F (160°C). Line a baking pan with parchment paper.

**2.** In a small bowl, whisk the egg. In a medium bowl, combine the nut butter, erythritol, butter, and vanilla extract. Add the egg and mix until a dough forms. Roll the dough into 6 balls. Place the balls in the pan and press them down with the back of a fork.

**3.** Place the pan in the fryer basket and bake until slightly golden around the edges, about 5 to 6 minutes. (Depending on the size of your fryer basket, you might need to bake the cookies in batches.)

**4.** Remove the pan from the fryer basket and allow the cookies to come to room temperature before serving.

 **Tips** Feel free to use any nut butter you like. I find that smooth nut butter works best. Store the baked cookies in an airtight container in the fridge for up to 7 days.

# Crème Brûlée

Traditional crème brûlée has a layer of caramelized sugar. This version is sugar-free and uses top-down heat from an air fryer to crisp the top to perfection.

**NUTRITION PER 1 RAMEKIN:**

**471** CALORIES
**47g** TOTAL FAT
**5g** NET CARBS
**6g** PROTEIN
**1g** DIETARY FIBER

PREP TIME
**10 mins**

COOK TIME
**25 mins**

MAKES
**2 ramekins**

SERVING SIZE
**1 ramekin**

2 egg yolks

2 tbsp erythritol sweetener, divided

1 cup heavy whipping cream

1 tsp vanilla bean paste

**1.** Set the air fryer on the bake setting and at 300°F (145°C).

**2.** In a medium bowl, whisk together the egg yolks and 1 tablespoon of erythritol until the mixture becomes creamy. Add the whipping cream and vanilla bean paste. Mix well.

**3.** Place an equal amount of the mixture into 2 ramekins and cover with aluminum foil. Place the ramekins on a baking pan and add water to the pan until it's halfway up the ramekins.

**4.** Place the pan in the fryer basket and bake until the mixture is firm, about 25 minutes.

**5.** Remove the pan from the fryer basket and allow the ramekins to come to room temperature. Refrigerate the ramekins overnight to allow the custard to set.

**6.** Remove the ramekins from the fridge and top each with an equal amount of the remaining 1 tablespoon of erythritol. Use a culinary torch to melt the erythritol. You can also place the ramekins in the fryer basket at 400°F (200°C) and cook until the erythritol is golden brown, about 1 minute, repeating as needed. Serve immediately.

 **Tips** If you're unable to get vanilla bean paste, use a good-quality vanilla extract or the seeds from a vanilla pod as alternatives. Store the baked crème brûlée in an airtight container in the fridge for up to 4 days.

# Vanilla & Berries Birthday Cake

This moist cake features cream cheese icing as well as strawberries and blueberries. It's a perfect treat for celebrating special occasions with family and friends.

**NUTRITION PER 1 SLICE:**

**260** CALORIES
**24g** TOTAL FAT
**4g** NET CARBS
**7g** PROTEIN
**3g** DIETARY FIBER

| PREP TIME | COOK TIME | MAKES | SERVING SIZE |
|---|---|---|---|
| **15 mins** | **27 mins** | **8 slices** | **1 slice** |

1 cup almond flour

¼ cup coconut flour

1 tsp baking powder

1½ tsp gelatin powder

¼ tsp sea salt

5 large eggs, whisked

½ cup granulated erythritol sweetener

¼ cup heavy whipping cream

½ cup unsalted butter (1 stick), melted

1 tsp pure vanilla extract

½ cup fresh blueberries

½ cup fresh strawberries, sliced

**for the icing**

1¼ cups full-fat cream cheese (10oz [285g])

2 tbsp heavy whipping cream

3 tbsp powdered erythritol sweetener

2 tsp pure vanilla extract

2 tsp freshly squeezed lemon juice

**1.** Set the air fryer on the bake setting and at 320°F (160°C). Line an 8-inch (20cm) cake pan with parchment paper.

**2.** In a medium bowl, combine the almond flour, coconut flour, baking powder, gelatin powder, and salt. Mix well.

**3.** In a separate medium bowl, combine the eggs, erythritol, whipping cream, butter, and vanilla extract. Add the dry ingredients to the wet ingredients and mix well. Pour this mixture into the pan.

**4.** Place the pan in the fryer basket and bake until a toothpick comes out of the middle clean, about 45 minutes. Check after 30 minutes to ensure no burning has occurred.

**5.** In another medium bowl, make the icing by combining the cream cheese, whipping cream, powdered erythritol, vanilla extract, and lemon juice.

**6.** Remove the pan from the fryer basket and allow the cake to cool completely. Remove the cake from the pan by inverting the pan onto a plate.

**7.** Slice the cake in half lengthwise and cover the bottom cake layer with one-third of the icing and half the blueberries and strawberries. Place the remaining cake layer on top and cover with the remaining icing and berries. Slice into 8 slices before serving.

 **Tips** Feel free to use any fresh berries. Raspberries and blackberries are perfect alternatives, and depending on how carb-conscious you are, you can also use tropical fruits. Store the baked cake in an airtight container in the fridge for up to 4 days.

# Chocolate Lava Cake

These lava cakes are a slow-cooked recipe made easy in the air fryer. The deliciously firm top layer and the creamy indulgent center leave you wanting more.

**NUTRITION PER 1 RAMEKIN:**

**365** CALORIES
**36g** TOTAL FAT
**3g** NET CARBS
**9g** PROTEIN
**3g** DIETARY FIBER

PREP TIME
**10 mins**

COOK TIME
**16 mins**

MAKES
**2 ramekins**

SERVING SIZE
**1 ramekin**

2oz (60g) unsalted butter

1oz (30g) heavy whipping cream

2 tbsp erythritol sweetener (or ¼ tsp stevia liquid)

3 tbsp unsweetened cocoa powder

2 large eggs

½ tsp pure vanilla extract

**1.** Set the air fryer on the bake setting and at 300°F (145°C).

**2.** In a baking pan, combine the butter, whipping cream, and erythritol. Place the pan in the fryer basket and cook until the butter melts, about 1 minute, stirring often. Remove the pan from the fryer basket.

**3.** In a medium bowl, whisk together the cocoa powder, eggs, and vanilla extract. Slowly add the butter to the egg mixture, whisking quickly until all the butter has been added. Place an equal amount of the mixture in 2 ramekins and cover with aluminum foil.

**4.** Place the ramekins in the fryer basket and cook until the tops have cooked, about 15 minutes, leaving a little uncooked mixture toward the bottom, which is self-saucing.

**5.** Remove the ramekins from the fryer basket. Serve immediately.

**Tips** Slowly combining the melted butter mixture into the whisked eggs is the key to a smooth consistency for this recipe. Because you don't want to end up with scrambled egg cups, go easily with this step. Store the baked cakes in an airtight container in the fridge for up to 4 days.

# Blueberry Cobbler

This gets delightfully sticky and thick—unlike any keto recipe you've tried. The berries and biscuits pair well with your favorite keto-friendly ice cream.

**NUTRITION PER ¼ CUP:**

**372** CALORIES
**30g** TOTAL FAT
**12g** NET CARBS
**8g** PROTEIN
**6g** DIETARY FIBER

PREP TIME
**10 mins**

COOK TIME
**30 mins**

MAKES
**1 cup**

SERVING SIZE
**¼ cup**

1 tbsp salted butter

2 cups blueberries

¼ cup erythritol sweetener

½ tsp lemon zest

½ tsp xanthan gum

½ tsp ground cinnamon

juice of ½ lemon

**for the topping**

1 cup almond flour

2 tbsp erythritol sweetener

1 tsp baking powder

½ tsp xanthan gum

¼ cup salted butter (½ stick), melted

1 tsp pure vanilla extract

1 large egg, whisked, divided

**1.** Set the air fryer temp to 320°F (160°C).

**2.** Place the butter on a baking pan. Place the pan in the fryer basket and cook for 1 minute.

**3.** Remove the pan from the fryer basket and add the blueberries, erythritol, lemon zest, xanthan gum, cinnamon, and lemon juice. Return the pan to the fryer basket and cook until the blueberries are soft and the lemon is fragrant, about 15 minutes, mixing every 5 minutes.

**4.** In a medium bowl, make the topping by combining the almond flour, erythritol, baking powder, and xanthan gum. Mix well. Add the butter, vanilla extract, and half the egg. Mix well until a dough forms.

**5.** Place the dough between two sheets of parchment paper and roll out until ¼ inch (0.5cm) thick. Use a drinking glass (or a 3½-inch [8cm] round cookie cutter) to cut the dough into round circles. Keep rolling the cut dough flat to create 8 circles.

**6.** Remove the pan from the fryer basket and place the rounds of dough on top of the blueberries. Brush with the remaining half of egg. Return the pan to the fryer basket and cook until golden brown on top, about 15 minutes.

**7.** Remove the pan from the fryer basket and allow the cobbler to cool for 5 minutes before serving.

 **Tips** You can also serve this with a dollop of whipping cream. Store the cooked cobbler in an airtight container in the fridge for up to 7 days or in the freezer for up to 2 months.

# Pumpkin Pie

Combine this versatile autumn vegetable with a few diverse spices and it just cries out to be wrapped in a flaky pastry and sent to sweet-tooth heaven.

**NUTRITION PER 1 SLICE:**

**238** CALORIES
**22g** TOTAL FAT
**4g** NET CARBS
**5g** PROTEIN
**4g** DIETARY FIBER

PREP TIME
**15 mins**

COOK TIME
**27 mins**

MAKES
**8 slices**

SERVING SIZE
**1 slice**

8oz (225g) pumpkin purée

1 large egg, whisked

½ tsp or 20 drops of stevia liquid

1½ tsp pumpkin spice

5 fl oz (150ml) heavy whipping cream

**for the crust**
3oz (90g) almond flour

1oz (30g) coconut flour

½ tsp xanthan gum

½ tsp baking powder

¼ tsp sea salt

3oz (90g) unsalted butter, chilled and cubed

**1.** In a food processor, make the crust by combining the almond flour, coconut flour, xanthan gum, baking powder, and salt. Pulse a few times to ensure the mixture is well combined. Add the butter and pulse 15 times or until the butter just combines with the flour and looks crumbly. Remove the dough from the food processor, wrap in plastic wrap, and refrigerate for 20 minutes.

**2.** Set the air fryer temp to 320°F (160°C).

**3.** Place the dough between two sheets of parchment paper and roll out until ¼ inch (0.5cm) thick. Place an 8-inch (20cm) pie pan over the top and flip to place the crust in the pan. Remove any dough hanging over the edge and poke holes in the bottom using a fork.

**4.** Place the pan in the fryer basket and bake until the edges are slightly golden brown, about 5 minutes.

**5.** In a medium bowl, combine the pumpkin purée, egg, stevia, and pumpkin spice. Mix well. Slowly add the whipping cream while mixing to ensure the cream mixes in evenly.

**6.** Remove the pan from the fryer basket and pour the pumpkin filling into the crust. Return the pan to the fryer basket and bake until the filling has set, about 10 minutes.

**7.** Remove the pan from the fryer basket and allow the pie to cool completely. Refrigerate overnight. Slice into 8 slices before serving.

 **Tips** If you don't have pumpkin spice, use ½ teaspoon of ground cinnamon, ½ teaspoon of ground ginger, and ½ teaspoon of ground nutmeg as a replacement. Store the baked pie in an airtight container in the fridge for up to 5 days or in the freezer for up to 2 months.

# Pecan Bars

This recipe combines the nutty texture from pecans with hints of maple and whiskey and a sweet blonde base. This treat pairs well with a warm cup of coffee.

PREP TIME
**10 mins**

COOK TIME
**18 mins**

MAKES
**10 bars**

SERVING SIZE
**1 bar**

⅓ cup almond flour

¼ cup chopped pecans

1 tbsp coconut flour

1½ tsp gelatin powder

⅓ cup unsalted butter, melted

1 large egg

¼ cup erythritol sweetener

1 tsp pure vanilla extract

1 tbsp sugar-free maple syrup

¼ tsp sea salt

**for the topping**

1 tbsp salted butter

½ cup roughly chopped pecans

¼ cup erythritol sweetener

2 tbsp sugar-free maple syrup

1 fl oz (30ml) whiskey

1 tsp pure vanilla extract

**1.** Set the air fryer on the bake setting and at 320°F (160°C). Line a baking pan with parchment paper.

**2.** On a separate baking pan, make the topping by combining the butter and pecans. Place the pan in the fryer basket and cook until the pecans are toasted, about 3 minutes.

**3.** Remove the pan from the fryer basket and add the erythritol, maple syrup, whiskey, and vanilla extract. Stir to combine. Set aside.

**4.** In a large bowl, make the blondie by combining the almond flour, pecans, coconut flour, and gelatin powder. In a separate large bowl, use a hand mixer to combine the melted, egg, erythritol, vanilla extract, maple syrup, and salt. Fold the dry ingredients into the wet ingredients. Pour the mixture into the lined pan.

**5.** Place the pan in the fryer basket and bake until lightly golden on top, about 5 minutes. Remove the pan from the fryer basket and top the blondie with the pecan mixture.

**6.** Return the pan to the fryer basket and bake until the pecans are lightly toasted, about 10 minutes more.

**7.** Remove the pan from the fryer basket and allow the blondie to cool. Refrigerate overnight. Slice into 10 slices before serving.

💬 **Tips** If you don't want to use the whiskey, simply leave it out. If you can't get sugar-free maple syrup, replace with the same quantity of erythritol. Store the baked bars in an airtight container in the fridge for up to 7 days or in the freezer for up to 2 months.

# Lemon Pound Cake

"Pound" cake comes from using a pound each of four ingredients, but I'll show you how to get the same buttery-rich texture without the sugar and extra carbs.

**NUTRITION PER 1 SLICE:**

**235** CALORIES
**22g** TOTAL FAT
**3g** NET CARBS
**8g** PROTEIN
**3g** DIETARY FIBER

PREP TIME
**15 mins**

COOK TIME
**30 mins**

MAKES
**8 slices**

SERVING SIZE
**1 slice**

½ cup salted butter (1 stick), melted

½ cup erythritol sweetener (4oz [120g])

3 large eggs

1½ cups almond flour

zest of 1 lemon

juice of 1 lemon

2 tsp baking powder

1 tbsp gelatin powder

**for the icing**

½ cup powdered erythritol sweetener

1 tbsp freshly squeezed lime juice

½ tsp lemon zest

**1.** Set the air fryer on the bake setting and at 315°F (155°C). Line an 8-inch (20cm) springform pan with parchment paper.

**2.** In a medium bowl, use a hand mixer to combine the butter and erythritol until lightly fluffy. Add the eggs and continue to beat until well combined.

**3.** Add the almond flour, lemon zest and juice, baking powder, and gelatin powder. Mix well. Place the mixture in the pan.

**4.** Place the pan in the fryer basket and bake for 30 minutes. Check for doneness by inserting a toothpick in the middle. If the toothpick comes out clean, the cake is done.

**5.** In a small bowl, make the icing by combining the powdered erythritol and lime juice. Mix until it resembles icing. Add more lime juice if the erythritol is too dry.

**6.** Remove the pan from the fryer basket and allow the cake to cool completely. Top with the icing and sprinkle the lemon zest over the top. Slice into 8 slices before serving.

 **Tips** Serve this with a scoop of keto-friendly ice cream or a dollop of whipping cream. Store the baked cake in an airtight container in the fridge for up to 7 days or in the freezer for up to 2 months.

# Blueberry Muffins

These are based on a favorite recipe from my blog. High in antioxidants, blueberries can help reduce DNA damage, lower blood pressure, and improve memory.

**NUTRITION PER 1 MUFFIN:**

**157** CALORIES
**14g** TOTAL FAT
**5g** PROTEIN
**4g** NET CARBS
**2g** DIETARY FIBER

PREP TIME
**10 mins**

COOK TIME
**15 mins**

MAKES
**7 muffins**

SERVING SIZE
**1 muffin**

1 cup almond flour
(4oz [120g])

1 tsp baking powder

2 large eggs

¼ tsp liquid stevia

2 tbsp almond milk

1 tsp pure vanilla extract

1 tsp olive oil

21 blueberries (about ⅓ cup)

**1.** Set the air fryer temp to 360°F (180°C).

**2.** In a medium bowl, combine the almond flour and baking powder. Ensure the baking powder is evenly distributed. Add the eggs, liquid stevia, almond milk, and vanilla extract. Mix well.

**3.** Line 7 silicone muffin liners (or a large round silicone muffin tray) with a little olive oil. (Using your index finger is the easiest way to spread the oil.) Fill each liner with 2 or 3 tablespoons of the mixture and ensure all liners are evenly filled. Place 3 blueberries on top of each filled liner and press down until they're level with the mixture.

**4.** Place the liners in the fryer basket and ensure they're level and not squished from the sides. Cook until firm all the way through and golden brown on top, about 17 minutes. Check for doneness by pressing the edges to look for any uncooked batter underneath.

**5.** Remove the muffins from the fryer basket and allow to cool for 5 minutes before serving.

**Tips** Placing the muffins on a flat surface in the air fryer is important to getting nice-looking muffins. I used a pizza pan lowered into the fryer basket using an aluminum foil sling. (See page 13.) You can also make these muffins with chocolate chips, walnuts, and even white chocolate and macadamias. Store the cooled baked muffins in an airtight container in the fridge for up to 7 days or in the freezer for up to 1 month.

# Biscotti

Biscotti is a twice-baked cookie. This recipe combines the zest of orange with the sweetness of cardamom and vanilla to create an exceptional air-fried dessert.

**NUTRITION PER 1 SLICE:**

**110** CALORIES
**10g** TOTAL FAT
**5g** NET CARBS
**4g** PROTEIN
**2g** DIETARY FIBER

PREP TIME
**15 mins**

COOK TIME
**21 mins**

MAKES
**12 slices**

SERVING SIZE
**1 slice**

½ cup raw almonds

2 tbsp unsalted butter, room temperature

¼ cup erythritol sweetener

1 large egg

¼ tsp ground cardamom

1 tsp orange zest

1 tsp pure vanilla extract

¾ cup almond flour

2 tbsp coconut flour

½ tsp xanthan gum

**1.** Set the air fryer on the bake setting and at 320°F (160°C). Line a baking pan with parchment paper.

**2.** Place the almonds in a single layer on a separate baking pan. Place the pan in the fryer basket and cook for 5 minutes. Remove the pan from the fryer basket and roughly chop the nuts. Set aside.

**3.** In a medium bowl, use an electric hand mixer to whisk together the butter and erythritol until light and fluffy. Add the egg, cardamom, orange zest, and vanilla extract. Mix well.

**4.** In a separate medium bowl, combine the almond flour, coconut flour, and xanthan gum. Add to the butter mixture and mix well. Add the almonds and mix again. Place the mixture in the pan and shape into an elongated roll.

**5.** Place the pan in the fryer basket and bake until golden brown on top, about 10 minutes. Remove the pan from the fryer basket and allow the roll to cool for 5 minutes. Slice the roll into 12 slices horizontally at a 45-degree angle.

**6.** Place the slices in the fryer basket and bake until brown on the edges and cooked through, about 6 minutes more, flipping halfway through. (Check regularly to ensure no burning occurs.)

**7.** Remove the biscotti from the fryer basket and allow to cool completely before serving.

 **Tips** If you have roasted almonds, skip to step 3. If you don't have xanthan gum, you can replace it with the same amount of guar gum or use ½ tablespoon of gelatin powder. Store the baked biscotti in an airtight container in the fridge for up to 7 days.

# New York–Style Baked Cheesecake

Because the air fryer operates in a similar fashion to an oven, you can make a New York baked cheesecake in this fabulous device—and it's worth the time.

**NUTRITION PER 1 SLICE:**

**300** CALORIES
**30g** TOTAL FAT
**7g** NET CARBS
**7g** PROTEIN
**2g** DIETARY FIBER

PREP TIME
**15 mins**

COOK TIME
**50 mins**

MAKES
**10 slices**

SERVING SIZE
**1 slice**

1 cup almond flour (5oz [140g])

¼ cup salted butter (½ stick), melted

2 tbsp plus ½ cup erythritol (or 10 drops plus ½ tsp liquid stevia)

1lb (450g) cream cheese, softened

½ cup sour cream (5oz [140g])

2 large eggs, divided

2 tsp pure vanilla extract

2 tbsp water

**1.** Set the air fryer on the bake setting and at 400°F (200°C). Line an 8.5-inch (22cm) springform pan with parchment paper.

**2.** In a medium bowl, combine the almond flour, butter, and 2 tablespoons of erythritol. Spread this mixture across the bottom of the cake pan and about 1 inch (2.5cm) up the sides.

**3.** Place the pan in the fryer basket and bake until the almond flour becomes fragrant, about 3 minutes. Remove the pan from the fryer basket and set aside.

**4.** Lower the air fryer temp to 300°F (150°C).

**5.** In a large bowl, combine the cream cheese, sour cream, 1 egg, and the remaining ½ cup of erythritol. Mix with an electric hand mixer or stand mixer until well combined.

**6.** Add vanilla extract, water, and the remaining 1 egg. Mix well. Place this batter on top of the almond flour mixture.

**7.** Place the pan in the fryer basket and bake until a skewer comes out clean from the middle, about 50 minutes.

**8.** Turn off the air fryer and allow the cheesecake to rest in the air fryer for 30 minutes to reach room temperature.

**9.** Remove the pan from the fryer basket. Remove the cheesecake from the pan and place in an airtight container. Freeze for at least 4 hours to set. Slice into 10 slices before serving.

 **Tips** If your air fryer doesn't have a bake setting, I'd suggest lowering the temp by 10 to 15°F (5 to 10°C) because the cheesecake needs to be cooked at a low temp to avoid cracking. Store the baked cheesecake in the fridge for up to 7 days or in the freezer for up to 2 months.

# Index

# About the Author

I'm Aaron Day and I run a popular ketogenic website called FatForWeightLoss. I'm an accredited nutritional therapist, dietary supplements advisor, sports exercise nutritional advisor, and clinical weight loss practitioner.

I'm also a professional recipe developer, food photographer, and videographer, all of which help me showcase my love for quick and simple keto-friendly meals.

Throughout my study, I researched and absorbed the world of nutrition, through which I realized I had a deeply rooted passion in helping others be able to live to their full potential. Whether I'm competing in cycling events or running marathons using the unusual endurance diet of high-fat, low-carb foods, I'm dedicated to pushing past what's generally deemed possible.

Through those ambitious goals, I've realized it's not the outcome that you learn the most from. It's the journeys and struggles along the way that make you become a better person. That is my guiding principle in all I do, including this book.

# Acknowledgments

While writing, testing, and eating my way through these recipes, there have been moments of complete joy and moments of complete disaster (so you don't have to make the same mistakes). These recipes represent a special piece of my life that, hopefully, you can pass on to your family, friends, and loved ones.

This book is dedicated to all my readers from FatForWeightLoss. Without your support and honest feedback, I wouldn't have been able to dedicate my life to creating such a helpful resource for others.

I'd like to thank my life partner, Adele Rose. Without your support, guidance, love, and cooking skills and experience, I wouldn't be where I am today. Thank you for teaching me everything I know in the kitchen and for giving me a level of excellence I couldn't have achieved by myself.

Thanks to my family, who taught me the joys of baking, mentored a life in pursuit of better health, and showed me how to harness my own passion and opportunity to create a business of my own.

I'd like to thank all the staff at DK and Alpha Books, including Christopher Stolle, and the fantastic recipe testers for making this project possible. I can't even imagine what this book would have been like without your help.

Thank you to my friends, who have kept me sane throughout the whole process but still aren't sure how I make a living.

*"It is good to have an end to journey toward; but it is the journey that matters, in the end."*
— Ursula K. Le Guin